P9-AQO-998

MASCULINE
IDENTITIES

MASCULINE IDENTITIES

THE HISTORY AND MEANINGS OF MANLINESS

Herbert Sussman

PRAEGER

AN IMPRINT OF ABC-CLIO, LLC
Santa Barbara, California • Denver, Colorado • Oxford, England

St. Charles Community College Library

Copyright 2012 by Herbert Sussman

All rights reserved. No part of this publication may be reproduced, stored in a retrieval system, or transmitted, in any form or by any means, electronic, mechanical, photocopying, recording, or otherwise, except for the inclusion of brief quotations in a review, without prior permission in writing from the publisher.

Library of Congress Cataloging-in-Publication Data

Sussman, Herbert L.
    Masculine identities : the history and meanings of manliness / Herbert Sussman.
        p. cm.
    Includes bibliographical references and index.
    ISBN 978-0-313-39159-0 (hardcopy : alk. paper) — ISBN 978-0-313-39160-6 (ebook)
1. Masculinity—History.   2. Men—History.   I. Title.
    HQ1090.S88   2012
    305.31—dc22   2011047144

ISBN: 978-0-313-39159-0
EISBN: 978-0-313-39160-6

16   15   14   13   12   1   2   3   4   5

This book is also available on the World Wide Web as an eBook.
Visit www.abc-clio.com for details.

Praeger
An Imprint of ABC-CLIO, LLC

ABC-CLIO, LLC
130 Cremona Drive, P.O. Box 1911
Santa Barbara, California 93116-1911

This book is printed on acid-free paper ∞

Manufactured in the United States of America

To
Henry, Owen, Jacob, Quill

Contents

Acknowledgments

The writing of a book depends upon exchange with others. Notably, the mention of masculinity evokes opinions from everyone. I would especially mention conversations on manliness with fellow Victorianists John Maynard, Adrienne Munich, and Carole Silver. And I have learned much about masculinities past and present in discussions with students at both Eugene Lang College of The New School and The New School for General Studies. And, as always, Elisabeth.

Thinking about Men

"Not all men are men." This paradox that we seldom think about but always act upon—not all men in the sense of persons born biologically male become "men" or "real men" living up to the socially constructed ideal set for males that we call manliness. As a value system set by individual societies, manliness takes different shapes in different cultures and changes over time. Men absorb these values in a script for ideal behavior as men that we call masculinity. From such scripts, men fashion for themselves a sense of themselves as men, a masculine identity.

We don't often think about manliness. Mostly we consider the behavior of men as simply natural. We often say, "That's the way men are." Occupied with behaving as real men, men seldom step outside the socially given ideals to consider alternatives, to see themselves as living within a discourse of masculinity that is historically specific and yet emerges from the history of manliness. Manliness is an unmarked category, an area that is seemingly so self-evident in its meaning that we seldom think about it. And when we do, we often meet confusion and contradiction. So it might be useful to set out some definitions, some issues, and some problems as we move to a history of masculine identities.

The Sex/Gender Distinction

We begin with a very basic distinction of great use, although the distinction runs against common usage. This is the sex/gender distinction. Here the term *sex* refers to the biological basis of self. A person is born within the male sex or the female sex, although, as we shall discuss, for some persons and in some cultures, even this sharp biological distinction can be problematic. *Gender,* on the other hand, describes the expectations or definitions established by society for behavior by persons of a specific sex.

In common usage, however, gender is often used for what we are here calling sex, as in the term *gender discrimination.* Perhaps this conflating of sex with gender is a way of avoiding the other common meaning of sex as sexuality. The term *gender discrimination* avoids the implication of sex discrimination as a violation of the codes of sexual conduct. Yet erasing the word *gender* also functions to repress the still rather subversive notion that the behavior of each sex is principally determined by social scripts. Whatever the case, this study will employ the word *sex* to refer to biology and *gender* to mean the social formation of the proper behavior for each sex.

The basic question posed by the sex/gender distinction troubles our thinking about men. Is sex identical with gender? For men, is behavior determined by the body into which males are born? To what degree is male action and feeling based in the body and to what extent learned or constructed by upbringing and social norms? Do men act as they do because of testosterone or because of their upbringing? Is the male brain wired to be good at math and rational thinking? Has evolution of the human species shaped men to be hunters, not gatherers nor nurturers? Are men hardwired to join fight clubs, or does society teach males to fight from their earliest moments?

The crucial lesson taught by the feminist movement has been to challenge the easy—and in many ways, destructive belief—in a necessary and inevitable link between sex and behavior. Being born within the female sex does not necessarily mean that women are naturally subservient to men, uncontrollably emotional, and poor at math. But we have been reluctant to apply this distinction to men. Men are still seen within a hormonal theory, as driven by testosterone. One of the prime efforts of this book is to apply the sex/gender distinction to men, to show that being born of the male sex does necessarily bring with it a set of skills such as being good at math and at building towers; or the desire to be violent, aggressive, and sexually domineering.

To preserve the sex/gender distinction in thinking about the complex relation of biology and behavior, this book will use the term *male* to refer to biology or sex, although, as we shall see, this category of the *male sex* dissolves on inspection. I will use the term *masculinity* and its plural *masculinities* as well as the noun *manliness* and the adjective of manliness, *manly,* to refer to gender, the social expectations for male behavior. *Manhood* refers to the state of an achieved manliness as an adult male, with the sense that such a state must be continuously maintained in the eyes of other men.

Essentialism vs. Social Construction

Thinking about men, then, engages the long-standing debate about nature vs. nurture. In the language of gender studies, the issue lies between essentialism, the theory that behavior is determined by innate biological qualities; and social construction, the belief that the behavior of each sex is constructed or shaped by the society. The issue in regard to men is extraordinarily difficult to resolve; many forms of evidence are marshaled. I will not attempt to resolve this question of essentialism vs. social construction here but rather try to clarify our thinking about the issue by describing the general forms the arguments take and noting some of the difficulties with each position.

There is the evidence of our own eyes. We see boys and men behaving the way we traditionally expect them to behave. In the everyday experience of even the most liberal families, little boys chase each other with big sticks or light sabers. Little girls sit demurely and play with dolls. Is this due to hardwired attachment to phallic weapons and the intense energy males are born with, or to an unnoticed valuing by parents of such masculine or feminine activities from the moment of birth? After all, the first question asked at birth is, "Is it a boy or a girl?" Gender typing starts from the beginning. Unfortunately, one cannot perform experiments with controls on infants, raising them differently to see if behavior is innate. Yet, as we shall see, the widely varying behavior of men in different cultures and subcultures, and in different historical moments, does suggest a strong element of social construction in shaping manliness.

In another form of argument, the defenders of essentialism employ an appeal to the animals, especially to the primates who are closest to the human species, to prove that sex-based qualities are biologically based. The males of our closest relatives, the chimpanzees, compete for domination and sexual partners and, we have recently learned, are warlike—killing and eating other chimpanzees in order to expand their territories. Thus it is argued, aggressive and violent conduct in men is validated as being natural.

There are several problems with this appeal to nature to show that certain styles of masculinity are innate. For one, animal studies have shown wide variations in the behavior of male and female animals. In the wild, some males exhibit traits traditionally marked as female. Some penguins stand guard over the penguin egg in the cold of the Antarctic. Chimps may kill other chimps, but bonobos, another primate species, head off conflict by turning to polymorphous sexual pleasure. Interestingly, the gorilla, the exemplar of primal ferocity as in the gigantic form of King Kong, turns out to be a vegetarian and his chest-beating, still employed by triumphal football players, a form of display to scare off enemies and thereby avoid conflict. Finally, even if certain aggressive behaviors of males are innate, passed on to the human species by genetic inheritance, does that validate or justify these behaviors? The process of civilization, one could argue, can be defined by rejecting the inheritance of a world red in tooth and claw.

A similar appeal to the natural invokes the evolution of innate sex-specific qualities as passed down in men and in women from the first days of the human species. This argument usually asserts that since the earliest times of homo sapiens, men were the hunters leaving the home to kill animals for food while women stayed behind to care for the children and cook the kill. Natural selection then created males who are physically strong and aggressive for hunting, defending the tribe, and expanding territory through war. Conversely, women's tasks called for a less robust physique but more developed nurturing skills and subordination to men. Extensive cross-cultural study of hunter-gatherer tribes does show this sexual division of labor with men as hunters and warriors as nearly universal.[1]

But what does the argument from human evolution and from cross-cultural findings about primitive tribes tell us about masculinities? There are several replies. The strongest may be that human society has changed; we are no longer hunter-gatherers. Primitive man lived as hunter and fighter because under the conditions of early human life, such roles for men were functional. And it must be emphasized, as we shall see, that the primary determinate for forms of masculinity lies in being functional or useful to the society. If certain skills and bodily forms did evolve in the past, new skills are evolving in the present as social needs change. In modern society, except in certain domains such as the armed forces or professional football, physicality is no longer functional for survival. Instead, within a technologically advanced corporate world, the skills needed by men are intellectuality and self-subordination within a corporate structure. Thus, the male body and mind is not natural but shaped by conditions. If in the distant past, the male physique was determined by the needs of war and hunting the giant mammoth, such a bodily form is certainly attenuated or made vestigial by sitting for hours in front of a computer screen. Only in the artifice of the gym can men maintain what some still feel is the natural male body. Indeed, the conflict between the masculine style of the hunter, seeming validated by the argument from evolution with the realities of male life today, accounts for much of the internal malaise of contemporary men.

Furthermore, this naturalizing of what are socially constructed phenomena has been constantly subverted by history. Even the most cursory view of the past and present shows what were once seen as truths about how biology has shaped men and women have been shattered by changes in gender as society changes. Feminism has called to consciousness the fallacies of using supposed facts about the essential nature of women to support historically specific cultural prejudices. Many in the nineteenth century believed that women have smaller brains than men and that studiousness in women would bring on female maladies. Recently, Lawrence Summers, as president of Harvard University, publicly stated that women were innately incapable of working at the highest levels of mathematics and science. This statement was one of the causes of his dismissal from his position. Of course, women now do superior work in engineering, mathematics, and science—even at Harvard.

As in the case of women, the essentialist view of manliness has weakened but remains remarkably persistent and generally unexamined, perhaps as a way of maintaining patriarchal power. A historical perspective and experience within our lifetimes shows manliness as constructed by culture and also changed by it. What has been seen as invariant and determined by the male body appears in the long view not as natural, but the result of unquestioned assumptions about ideal male behavior. We have seen new forms of masculine behavior become functional and therefore possible. Men no longer have to hunt game to support their families nor go on war parties to extend their tribal territory or bring back female slaves. We have seen the behavior of many men moving toward qualities once identified as innately female. In contemporary America society, men are expected to be dads: to be nurturing to their children, as well as sensitive to their wives.

In general, then, there are several concerns to be kept in mind when thinking about the relation between innateness and social construction in the formation of manliness. For one, the all-too-common generalizations that begin "all men are . . ." or similar statements that state "all women are . . ." certainly are inaccurate, if not destructive. Both sexes exhibit a wide range of behaviors. Not all women do math well; not all men nurture well, nor fight well. Finally, the actions and the feelings of men most likely emerge from a complex mix of the bodily and the cultural that has yet to be teased out in its particulars. Neither strict essentialism nor strict constructionism appears adequate for thinking about men. Rather than trying to resolve the issue of nature vs. nurture for men, a middle ground is probably the best territory to occupy.

Is Everybody Either a Man or Woman?:
The Two-Sex Model and Masculinity

I began this study by pointing to the double meaning of the term *man* as a biological category of sex and as gender, a term of cultural validation in meeting the social ideal of male behavior. And yet the more closely we examine the apparently self-evident biological definition of *man*, the more we see culture intruding. We believe, or wish to believe, that there are two and only two sexes. A man is defined both biologically and culturally as not a woman. The idea that there are only two sexes, two biological categories in to which all people must fit, is called the two-sex model. This dualism is built into the English language; our pronoun structure is limited to *he* or *she*. And yet on examination, this two-sex binary appears to be as much a product of social construction as of nature. It turns out that the division of humanity in only two categories, male and female is not a self-evident account of nature but a fairly recent invention.[2] The Greeks were quite happy with a one-sex model. For Aristotle there was only the male sex and the female as a person lacking male organs. The female was thus a secondary species, as befitting her subordinate place in society, rather than a separate sex with a unique biological makeup.

Furthermore, there are cases, limited ones perhaps, where the strict biological distinction between the male and female sex dissolves to reveal the cultural basis of the two-sex model. Sports, for example, are divided according to the dualism of sex. There is women's track, and there is men's track, men's weightlifting and women's weightlifting. Participants must be divided into male and female so as to compete in the proper category. But at the boundary, such classification becomes the stuff of controversy. Take the case of Caster Semenya, a South African runner who has competed in world-class events as an athlete. Because of her success, opponents claimed that Semenya was really a male and demanded testing. The international organization governing track compelled Semenya to undergo medical testing that concluded she could participate as a woman.[3] The details of the physical testing remain confidential. Semenya has continued to run with great competitive success as a woman.

The case of Semenya illustrates the difficulty of fitting runners or weightlifters or tennis players into the either/or categories of male or female. Once the two-sex model is put into play, the medical criteria for determining whether a person is a male or female is complex and problematic, depending less on physical evidence than on the social definition as to what biological markers define a man as opposed to a woman. For example, many persons are born with a mix of male and female sexual organs: for example, an ovary and a penis.[4] The birth of such persons of mixed biological sex, such as infants, with what is called a "micropenis," a penis below normal size, or a mix of sexual organs, presents an agonizing issue for parents. Should surgery on the infant be done to make the child a girl or a boy? Some argue that such a procedure will allow the child to function in a society in which one must be either male or female to lead a normal life. But there is also a strong movement for doing nothing, of allowing the person to become an intersex person, a term replacing the older term hermaphrodite— combining both male and female sexes.[5] Medical science, then, cannot resolve the vexing question of how to classify athletes or whether to perform urological surgery on intersex babies. The success of the recent novel *Middlesex* by Jeffrey Eugenides shows public acceptance that an intersex person, a person of a middle sex, can lead a rich life. The difficulty of determining sex in limited cases such as intersex infants suggests that here, as in other issues that we will discuss, it is more accurate to employ the model not of duality but of a continuum. Here, seeing a continuity between male and female, rather than working with difficulty to enforce a boundary would be more attuned to nature and eliminate many false dilemmas and a good deal of physical and emotional pain.

The intersex person challenges the two-sex model of male/female in another way. To the two-sex model and the one-sex model can be added the third-sex model. Many societies in the past and in the present accept as natural and normal a person who does not fit the rigid model of male or female. Many Native American tribes acknowledge a *berdache,* often called a "two-spirit" person, who contains the spirit of both the male and the female, and who often serves as a shaman. As we shall see, toward the end of the nineteenth century in Europe, males who were attracted to other men were thought of not as males with a perverse choice of sexual objects but as a "third sex": women trapped within a male body. In contemporary Brazil, a third-sex categorization applies to certain males who engage in male-male sexual relations. As the author of the study of such third-sex persons notes, sex categories "should be seen not as consisting of men and women, but rather of men and not-men, the latter being a category into which both biological females and males who enjoy anal penetration are culturally situated."[6]

Although challenged by the intersex movement as well as by historical and cross-cultural evidence, the two-sex binary persists in the general thinking about men in spite of its destructive bodily and psychological effects. Urological surgery on infants with mixed markers of sex would not be an issue unless there were a drive to make such children normal within the two-sex model. For adults, the desire to be either male or female as defined by cultural criteria imposes destructive psychic costs. Michel Foucault in his account of a hermaphrodite in nineteenth-century France illustrates the emotional pain created by prejudice against the intersex person.[7] So we can ask why, in the face of this devastation, do we see this intense investment in maintaining this two-sex model with its sharp line for the biological definition of men? One answer would be that if there were no men, there would be no masculinity. After all, it is still a world in which the biologically defined group called men still holds power. Such a group can only exist if we can tell who is a male and who is not one. Patriarchy as a system of authority depends on the two-sex model.

Manliness as Performance

Once manliness is seen as a social construction, another model emerges that is quite productive in thinking about men. This is the theory of gender as performance or, in the language of gender studies, as performative. Rather than being born with a set of innate qualities, the male at birth is a clean slate. Yet at birth society presents each male with a script that he must perform consistently and in all circumstances—in the locker room, at work, and with women—to show that he is a "real man." As Judith Butler, the foremost proponent of this theory states, "The view that gender is performative sought to show that what we take to be an internal essence of gender is manufactured through a sustained set of acts, posited through the gendered stylization of the body. In this way, it shows that what we take to be an 'internal' feature of ourselves is one that we anticipate and produce through certain bodily acts."[8]

The sense of manliness as continuous unbroken performance highlights the pressure on men to keep to the script, to follow the code—not to break character—for any divergence would show that one is not a true man but womanly or even gay. In its most radical form, such a model suggests that there is nothing natural or innate in men, perhaps not what we commonly call a "self." For men there is only a set of socially constructed rules for playing a role. Furthermore, the idea of manliness as performative also suggests what the history of manliness shows: if the social script is changed the behavior of men will change. This book will mark a number of such transformations.

Masculinity as Identity

We commonly use the term "identity" to mean our own sense of self of who we are. But to be a self in isolation is neither possible nor sustainable. For men a sense of self, consciously or unconsciously, has been, and continues to be, created by affiliating with other men in a shared identity, in a larger social construction in which the individual takes part and from which he draws his own sense of value. For example, America has recently seen a rise in "identity politics" in which individuals shape their own lives by their association with a formerly marginalized group. One achieves an identity by merging with and identifying with other selves. Thus, within identity politics, a man might say "I am a Latino," or "I am a gay American," or "I am an African American." In ancient Athens, a man might say with justifiable pride, "I am a citizen of Athens," thereby defining himself honorifically as having certain attributes of the self that he shares with other free-born men of the city-state. A contemporary American man might say, "I am a Marine" to define his life-long shared identity with his fellows in the Corps—"Once a Marine, always a Marine."

I have titled this book *Masculine Identities* to focus on the varied way that in different times and places, a man fashions a self—an identity—by linking his own being to other men within a collective social ideal or script that defines manliness.

One final note. For the sake of clarity, this book parses out single or pure identities for men—warrior, craftsman, bourgeois businessman, African American, Jewish American, and gay. But I must emphasize that the variants and possibilities of manliness are manifold. If we consider only contemporary America, the book does not, for example, consider how scripts of manliness are inflected by social class (working-class, middle-class, old wealth), by region (New England, Texas, Midwest), or ethnicity (Latino, Chinese, Japanese, Korean, Italian). Furthermore, in real life, masculine identities within a single person almost always take a hybrid form in combining multiple scripts into innumerable forms of a life of manliness. Modern American offers, to take only a few examples, African-American corporate titans; Jewish boxers; and gay tennis champions.

Chapter 1

Man as Warrior

In Homer's *Iliad,* the great Western epic of man as warrior, Hector, the champion of the besieged Trojans, finds himself outside the city walls and facing Achilles, the champion of the Greeks, a fighter that none can stand against. Hector's wonderful soliloquy ponders whether to retreat to the safety of the city or meet certain death in single combat with Achilles. His words eloquently summarize the code of the warrior that motivates Hector as well as Achilles and continues into our own time.

Hector wavers, then runs. Achilles chases him around the walls of Troy until taunted by Achilles to prove himself "a daring man of war" (22: 318). Hector finally stands, knowing full well that he will die in combat:

> My time has come!
> At last the gods have called me down to death . . .
> So now I meet my doom. Well, let me die—
> but not without struggle, not without glory, no,
> in some great clash of arms that even men to come
> will hear of down the years. (22: 350–51; 359–63)[1]

Resolved to die as a man of honor, Hector enters fully into his identity as a warrior, transcending self to lose the self in the frenzy of battle rage that marks the warrior:

> And on
> that resolve
> he [Hector] drew the whetted sword that hung at his side,
> tempered, massive, and gathering all his force
> he swooped like a soaring eagle
> launching down from the dark clouds to earth
> to snatch some helpless lamb or trembling hare.

So Hector swooped now, swinging his whetted sword
and Achilles charged too, bursting with rage, barbaric,
guarding his chest with the well-wrought blazoned shield. (22: 363–70)

Hector does indeed perish, his throat cut by the spear of Achilles, but he achieves the warrior's death: "glory, in some great clash of arms" as to this day we listen to and read with admiration Homer's words.

This paradigmatic episode that men "hear of down the years" encapsulates vividly in word and action the warrior identity. A true warrior will spurn the safety of a domestic life within the walls of the city. His greatest fear is to be shamed publicly before other men, even, as in the case of Hector, to be shamed before his greatest enemy, Achilles. Honor is the warrior's greatest good and death before dishonor his motto. His performance of this identity depends on his physical prowess and martial skill. The most intense realization of his essential self lies in battle rage as a reversion from civilized man to animal, a "soaring eagle," and, given the Greek and Trojan sense of themselves as civilized, in a turn to the "barbaric." Paradoxically, the true finding of self lies in moments of losing this self through killing other men. An honorable death achieves a new life in the eternal singing of the warrior's name and deeds by generations of bards.

It is this basic code that runs through the lives of men as warriors from Homeric times to the Greek city-state of Sparta, to the samurai of feudal Japan, to the Christian knights of the European Middle Ages, to the German fascists of the twentieth century, to the elite fighting units of our time such as the United States Marine Corps, to American professional football players who perform for the vicarious pleasure of the male TV audience.

The Warrior and Society

The warrior is an individual, but, as with all forms of masculine identity, he derives this identity from the values and structures of the society into which he is born. Yet, as we shall see, the cultural ethos of the warrior is remarkably similar across cultures.

All masculine identities survive because they are functional and serve the purpose of the society at large. Almost all societies need fighters to defend and expand the tribe or the city-state or the nation; yet the importance of the warrior within a society varies. We can consider this social significance of the warrior to his society along a continuum. At one pole would be warrior societies in which warriors do not form a separate male group but encompass all males within the society. Every male is a warrior. The Homeric tribes consist primarily of fighters but with some champions, like Hector and Achilles, who engage in heroic single combat. The exemplar of the warrior state is ancient Sparta, a polity whose main occupation is warfare and in which all male citizens are fashioned as soldiers from boyhood and live their adult lives as warriors with other men. In a culture devoted to raiding and pillaging, such as the Apaches or the Vikings, all men are fighters.

Although warfare is present in almost all cultures, fighting is not necessarily the occupation of all men. Often, warriors form a separate caste serving under the control of the ruler. Such warrior castes are exemplified by the samurai of preindustrial Japan who served the lords of small competing domains or the Christian knights of the European Middle Ages under the command of their feudal lord. Empires have employed warrior tribes within the imperium for the purposes of controlling the population. The Russian czars employed the Cossacks, a people from the Russian border with Asia famous for their skill as cavalrymen, to enforce their rule well into the time of the Russian Revolution of 1917. The British turned both the Gurkhas, an ethnic group from Nepal, and the Sikhs, a warlike sect, as separate military units to maintain their imperial rule within India. The Gurkhas still fight within the British Army as an elite unit, yet always under the command of British officers.

A warrior caste may be functional, but the problem lies in its control. For cultures devoted to other purposes and other value systems, as in such democracies as ancient Athens, America, and England—where defense and imperial expansion remain secondary functions within the state—the committed fighter poses a danger to the sovereignty of civil authority whether of a civilian assembly, an elected president, or a parliament. We see in our world too many military takeovers of civilian states. In the direct democracy of Athens, the assembly of citizens had the power to appoint and dismiss generals, as well as to ratify or reject on war plans. The founding document of the United States—the Constitution—demonstrates the founding fathers' fear of the power of a warrior caste in its inclusion of one of the most effective principles of our governance: the civilian control of the military. The president is the commander in chief. The elite units of the American military such as the Marines, a contemporary American warrior caste, operate under the control of civilian authority.

Another means of limiting the power of the warrior caste is to make all men warriors by creating an army in which all men serve but only for a set period and in times of emergency. This creation of citizen soldiers, wherein fighting is a part but not the whole of each man's identity, prevents the rise of a warrior caste that might seize power for itself. A citizen whose primary identity lies in civilian life as craftsman or politician or businessman can set this civilian identity aside in times of war and then cast off his sense of himself as fighter after military service. A man is a warrior only for a time; this is not his essential identity. Being a warrior is a duty, not one's essential being. In democratic Athens, for example, all citizens were expected to serve in the phalanx for ground warfare or in the powerful Athenian navy. Even the philosopher Socrates served in the Athenian militia and was praised for his warrior qualities of enduring the hardship of a campaign and loyalty to his comrades.[2] Such modern democracies as Switzerland and Israel have citizens armies in which all men serve, and in the case of Israel, all women also serve. In the major wars of American history, citizens have been drafted to fight, taking their democratic and egalitarian values into the armed forces and then returning to civilian life. Yet the abandonment of the draft in contemporary America and the establishment of an all-volunteer military have generated fears of the emergence of a professional warrior caste separate from civilian society and exerting undue influence.

In general, the warrior as a heroic individual of extraordinary physical strength and martial skill—the champions of the Trojan War, the berserker of the Vikings, the samurai knight, the medieval Christian knight—has become less central to the fighting of wars. The elite warrior castes in United States military such as in the Navy SEALS and the Marines or the Special Air Service (SAS) of England may be essential for covert missions and especially dangerous actions, yet the combatant of exceptional training and fighting skill has been gradually marginalized. There are several reasons for the decline in the martial power of the individual warrior since the days of Homer. The primary cause lies in developments in military technology, particularly the use of gunpowder. The gun was the great equalizer of martial prowess, killing not only warriors but also their values. Victory no longer depends upon the skill of combatants with spear and sword at close quarters. A single soldier with a gun could, quite simply, kill at a distance the enemy armed with spear and sword. Hand-to-hand combat became rare. And yet, the warrior code with its valuing of bravery and fearlessness persisted even as gunnery improved. In the American Civil War, ranks on both sides walked bravely across open fields toward soldiers with repeating rifles, just as British soldiers led by their officers throughout World War I strode across no-man's-land against machine guns. Predictably, most of them died.

Furthermore, by the eighteenth century, fighting in the West was no longer the task of an elite caste whose entire lives were devoted to the military. Rather, there emerged the mass army of conscripts in total war. After the French Revolution of 1789, Napoleon had the citizens of the new nation-state drafted for a total war of nation against nation. The mass army of Napoleon or Frederick the Great of Prussia (ruled 1740–1786) depended on drill to form ordinary soldiers into a smoothly functioning machine in which individual skill and initiative were subordinated to the movements of overwhelming manpower. The victory was not won by champions in single combat but by the maneuvers of a mass army. Just as mechanized mass production deskilled and dissolved the identity of the craftsman, so the mass army led to a deskilling of the fighter and challenged his identity as a warrior.

Until recently, the identity of the warrior has been open only to men. There have been myths about female warriors such as the Amazons, a tribe of women who fight men and have cut off their right breast in order to operate their bows more smoothly. This purported amputation suggests the basic patriarchal notion that the female body is not adapted to warfare, and only the removal of the defining female body part can transform the woman into a warrior. In the first days of World War II, the comic book *Wonder Woman* began showing an Amazon woman and her band of women warriors. Wonder Woman was armed with bullet-rejecting bracelets and an invisible airplane so as to enter the world of men to fight the Axis powers. The descendents of Wonder Woman continue to this day in TV and animated cartoons.

With the growth of feminism, women warriors in popular and in high culture have multiplied. Noteworthy here is the wonderful memoir by Maxine Hong Kingston, *Woman Warrior,* wherein a young Chinese-American woman living in a traditionally patriarchal working-class family in California in the 1950s fantasizes about another life in which she trains as a Chinese master fighter who destroys the patriarchal power structure.[3] The film *Crouching Tiger, Hidden Dragon* about a female Zen warrior achieved huge commercial and critical success and was nominated for the Academy Award for Best Picture. And that is not to mention the innumerable Hollywood films and TV shows featuring female assassins of marvelous fighting skill. Yet such woman-warrior fantasies are but fictional visions of the new reality that women are indeed slowly being accepted into armed forces globally, particularly since warfare, as noted, no longer depends of physical strength. In America, women can now enter the military academies and volunteer to serve in the armed forces, although, as in Israel, they are still in theory, but not in practice, excluded from the dangers of combat.

The Warrior Code

Whether the ethos of a totalized warrior society or of a fighting caste within a more complex social order, the warrior code is remarkably uniform over history and across cultures. From the Homeric world to twenty-first-century America, from the Vikings to the samurai to the medieval knights, warriors follow a similar ethos and derive their identity from living out the warrior code. Indeed, performing the warrior code is the basis of their sense of self. Dying, according to this code, means an eternal life as one's heroic actions will be praised in song through all time. Social death would come with betraying the code and the consequent exclusion from the company of warriors. This universality and persistence of the warrior identity attests to its effectiveness as a social ideal in fashioning effective fighting men who willingly choose to die while protecting their tribe or nation.

At the heart of the warrior identity is the quest for honor, for reputation, for glory, for renown in the eyes of his fellow warriors. Personal honor as performing an unwritten code exists most easily in a shame culture—that is, a society where one's actions and sense of personal worth are regulated by the threat of negative opinions from one's peers and by the further penalty of expulsion from the community of men. Such a society differs from a law culture where laws are codified and punishment administered equally to all by the state. As one example, there is no government law requiring that a U.S. Marine risk his life to recover the body of a fallen comrade, only the expectations from his fellow Marines and his internalization of the need to maintain his honor and that of the Corps.

Personal honor, then, is central to warrior identity. We can list, briefly, certain other elements of this virtually universal warrior identity:

- physical courage peaking in a loss of rational self in a frenzied battle rage
- martial prowess, especially with hand weapons such as the sword, developed through long training
- unwavering loyalty to a master, whether tribal king or feudal lord or American president
- intense loyalty, even to death, to fellow warriors
- intense affective and even sexual bonds with other men of the warrior caste
- subordination, even repudiation of heterosexual bonds
- personal life of asceticism
- disdain for commercial activity, even for farming

To see how this warrior identity is manifested over time and across cultures in a consistent pattern, we will examine several cultures—feudal Japan's samurai, a warrior caste living according to the code of Bushido; ancient Sparta, a martial society in which all men are warriors; and contemporary America where warrior castes, such as the Marine Corps, occupy an ambiguous position.

Japanese Samurai

Let us look first at a warrior caste and warrior code that still occupies the contemporary imagination: the samurai warrior and his code of Bushido, a code similar to the chivalric ethos of the medieval Christian knight. The original samurai comprised a social order of skilled fighters that developed in twelfth-century Japan and continued to exert power into the nineteenth. Like most warriors, samurai occupied an aristocratic position within the society: lower than the king but above the peasant class, and obligated to serve their lords (*daimyo*). Much like the knights of medieval Europe, these men functioned as an elite fighting force for the lords of a feudal system who controlled small separate regions under the general authority of the ruler of Japan, the shogun. Their sense of self, then, depended on absolute loyalty to their superior. A letter from 1412 CE stressing the importance of duty to one's master was required reading for Japanese samurai in the Middle Ages, as well as for Japanese soldiers in World War II:

> First of all, a samurai who dislikes battle and has not put his heart in the right place even though he has been born in the house of the warrior, should not be reckoned among one's retainers. . . . It is forbidden to forget the great debt of kindness one owes to his master and ancestors and thereby make light of the virtues of loyalty and filial piety. . . . It is forbidden that one should . . . attach little importance to his duties to his master . . . There is a primary need to distinguish loyalty from disloyalty and to establish rewards and punishments.[4]

There were also samurai without masters called ronin. Such masterless warriors roamed Japan seeking a new lord and thereby an outlet for their martial expertise. The ronin are celebrated in Japanese folk stories and in the Japanese film *Seven Samurai* by Akira Kurosawa based on these tales. In the popular American adaptation of *Seven Samurai, The Magnificent Seven,* itinerant skilled fighters of the Old West protect a Mexican village against bandits. Indeed, the "have gun will travel" roaming gunfighters of American legend are the American equivalent of the ronin.

Like the medieval knights, as a highly disciplined and loyal force, the samurai were essential in a feudal society where small groups waged constant battles of territorial expansion and defense. But in the 1600s when the shogun strengthened control over the nation, the continuous warfare fought by professional warriors declined. As Japan entered an era of internal peace, the warrior function of the samurai faded as did the power and position of their caste. The samurai maintained their identity but not their function. Furthermore, when the isolation of Japan ceased in the mid-nineteenth century, the modern technology of rifles and machine guns spread through the kingdom, making the samurai method of warfare with sword obsolete. But the samurai, wanting a return to their role, staged a rebellion in the 1870s. Outnumbered by government troops, the samurai committed ritual suicide. And although the caste no longer exists in legal terms, the ideals persist in Japanese culture, even into the Japanese army of World War II.

The samurai ethos is defined in the code of Bushido. Although the code has had many incarnations over the centuries, the essential elements remain clear. As with all forms of the warrior ethos, Bushido aims to define not only actions but, more importantly, shape a totalizing identity. Like the unwritten rules of honorable warfare in the Homeric world or the code of chivalry in the European Middle Ages, Bushido seeks to both intensify fighting skill and yet contain the aggression and violence of the warrior. The samurai must maintain rectitude and follow reason and the law even at the cost of death. Courage is not an end in itself but must serve the cause of the right. For all of our contemporary emphasis on samurai swordplay, the ideal samurai warrior resembles the Christian knight in practicing mercy and benevolence, politeness and sincerity.

Yet like all warriors, in battle the samurai was to be fearless, unafraid of death. Strongly influenced by Zen Buddhism, the samurai code embodied a Zen-like paradox: acceptance of death in battle will keep one from death.

> Those who are reluctant to give up their lives and embrace death are not true warriors. . . . Go to the battlefield firmly confident of victory, and you will come home with no wounds whatever. Engage in combat fully determined to die and you will be alive; wish to survive in the battle and you will surely meet death. When you leave the house determined not to see it again you will come home safely; when you have any thought of returning you will not return. You may not be in the wrong to think that the world is always subject to change, but the warrior must not entertain this way of thinking, for his fate is always determined.[5]

Contrary to the contemporary idealization of the samurai as almost magically skilled in close combat, these Japanese knights used an early form of the rifle—the arquebus—introduced by Europeans; and starting in the late 1500s, they employed canons in battle. With the decline of civil war, these weapons were phased out as violating samurai honor. Yet the main weapon of the samurai, as for other warriors, his instrument for killing, the symbol of his identity, and the device for his own death was the sword. Like King Arthur's Excalibur, the samurai sword not only decided the battle but was the emblem of a man's identity as a warrior. When a young samurai was about to be born, a sword was brought into the birth chamber. Upon reaching the age of thirteen, in his coming-of-age ceremony, a male child symbolically entered manhood by being given his first real weapons and armor, and an adult name. Thus he became, thus he *was* a samurai. When the time came for an old samurai to die—and cross over into the "White Jade Pavilion of the Afterlife"—his honored sword was placed by his side.

Samurai swords were astonishing implements for the warrior, worthy of their continued celebration. They were of two kinds. The *katana*, carried by Japanese officers into World War II, is a curved, slender, single-edged blade with a long grip to accommodate two hands. These swords, able to cut through armor and flesh, were fashioned by traditional methods of blending and tempering different metals. Four metal bars—a soft iron bar to guard against the blade breaking, two hard iron bars to prevent bending, and a steel bar to take a sharp cutting edge—were all heated at a high temperature, then hammered together into a long rectangular bar that would become the sword blade. When the swordsmith ground the blade to sharpen it, the steel took the razor-sharp edge, while the softer metal ensured the blade would not break.[6]

Samurai also possessed a smaller sword, a dagger called a *wakizashi*. The *wakizashi* itself was a samurai's honor weapon and purportedly never left his side. He would sleep with it under his pillow, and it would be taken with him when he entered a house since had to leave his main weapons outside. It was with the *wakizashi* that the warrior would take the head of an honored opponent after killing him. It was also with the *wakizashi* that a samurai would ritually disembowel himself in the act of *seppuku*, or hara-kiri.[7]

For the samurai, as for other warriors, victory in battle demanded reaching a state of mind that transcends the self-consciousness and rationality of ordinary life: one that moves beyond reason and thoughtfulness into instinct. Rather than seeking the rage of Achilles or the Norse berserkers in battle, influenced by Zen Buddhism, the samurai in his training sought the Zen state of clearing the mind: of moving beyond thought through extensive training and apprenticeship that teaches not only specific martial skills but reshapes the self. The goal, then, of striking without thinking was at the heart of instruction. In the deadly art of swordplay, there is no time for thinking. For a samurai to hesitate before striking, even for the time it takes to blink an eye, would give his opponent time to deal the mortal blow. The key to wielding a sword in a lightning stroke lay in the Zen strategy of emptying the mind of everything that did not have to do with the task at hand. The mind must be clear. Once this state of mind was achieved, the warrior-to-be could become intent on learning the use of the sword with a single-minded concentration.

The most distinctive element of the samurai code, and the element that also lives in the popular imagination, is the ritualization of death before dishonor in *seppuku* or hara-kari. The reasons for self-destruction are many. To follow Bushido, a samurai who falters in battle must kill himself to atone for this dishonor. Or a samurai may commit *seppuku* on the battle-field to avoid capture in defeat. In certain instances, the *daimyo* may order his fighter to commit *seppuku*.

The act was highly ritualized. In a planned *seppuku*, rather than one per-formed on a battlefield, the samurai was bathed, dressed in a white robe, and fed his favorite meal. When he was finished with this preparation, his *wakizashi* was placed on his plate. Dressed ceremonially, with his sword placed in front of him and sometimes seated on special cloths, the warrior would prepare for death by writing a death poem. In the final action, the samurai plunged his own short dagger into his abdomen, moving the blade back and forth in disembowelment because the Japanese felt that the intes-tines were the seat of the emotions and the soul itself. Then, in great pain, the samurai stretched out his neck for an assistant in a task of great honor to decapitate him.

The ritual of *seppuku* exemplifies the warrior code. In keeping with the modes of a shame society rather than a law society, the warrior inflicts pun-ishment on himself as the ultimate form of restoring honor—rather than giving himself to the state for punishment. Such an honorable act is a sign of status, as only samurai were permitted to perform *seppuku*. And the act is seen as a destruction of the male body, an actual slicing of it. The act testi-fies to the control of mind and body even in great pain. Only a true warrior could commit *seppuku*. Although officially abolished in the 1870s in Japan, the practice continued in the Japanese military through World War II, where many Japanese soldiers and officers committed *seppuku* rather than surrender. At the bloody battle for Okinawa, rather than surrender, most defeated Japanese committed *seppuku* by jumping off the high cliffs of the island into the Pacific.

The twentieth-century Japanese author Yukio Mishima provides an intense and sympathetic account of *seppuku* in the modern world as continuing Japanese tradition in his story "Patriotism."[8] In this highly erotic and sensuous tale, a young officer kills himself at home after a failed military coup. Mishima himself attempted to revive the samurai tradition in Japan. In 1970, with a few companions, he attempted a coup d'état to restore the rule of the emperor. After the coup failed, he committed *seppuku* according to the warrior practice: having a companion behead him after he had cut his own abdomen.

For the samurai, the quest for honor, battle, life, and ritual death took place within an all-male society. Although there might be an arranged marriage with a woman of suitable rank, there was nothing of the domesticity so prized by middle-class men of our time. Affective bonds were with male peers; personal worth lay in avoiding shame in their eyes. As in the formation of other warrior castes, intense male bonding began in youthful training through ties forged between young samurai and their mentors. Sometimes these male-male relations were overtly physical as in the martial education of young Spartans. In most instances, the bonds were more of a passionate friendship. Such male-male ties, often informed by homoeroticism as in other warrior castes, eased the passing on of traditions and skills and enabled the sense of keen loyalty and self-sacrifice essential to warriors in battle.

Sparta, a Warrior Society

In feudal Japan, the samurai formed an elite warrior caste. Other men pursued other activities such as farming or commerce. In ancient Sparta, a Greek city-state flourishing in the fourth and fifth centuries BCE, not merely an elite caste, but the entire free-born male population lived as warriors and as warriors only. For Spartan men, being a warrior was their entire being and entire identity. No male Spartan farmed or traded or ran a business. The business of Sparta was war. And all Spartans were full-time warriors.

Such a warrior state differs from a society with a citizen-army, such as Switzerland or Israel, in which all men take army training and form a reserve corps but where the primary identity of men lies in their civilian roles in business or their professions. Spartan citizens were prohibited from business or commerce or even farming. They had no being outside of war, just as Achilles or Hector had no other identity beyond that of a fighter. In Sparta, the crafts and businesses were run by resident noncitizens and, to a limited extent, by the warriors' wives. Of the population of the city-state, the vast proportion were slaves (helots) who performed the onerous manual work of the city and the farm.

The complete shaping of body and soul into the warrior identity that *is* the man was accomplished by a severe system. A male child born as a citizen was examined at birth, and if there were any physical defects that could compromise his battle skills in later life, the infant was left in the wilderness to die. At the age of seven, the boy who had been allowed to live entered the all-male world that he was to inhabit for the rest of his life. He was taken from his family to undergo the totalizing Spartan education system called *agoge*. The Spartan boy lived in communal halls with other young men so as to establish affective life-long bonds to his fellows, rather than to his family. In this stage, the boy was given only one garment: a red cloak. He was fed little so as to be constantly hungry and encouraged to steal food to survive. If stealing was encouraged, being caught was punished. An apocryphal story epitomizes the Spartan ethic of enduring pain rather than dishonor. A boy who has stolen a fox is caught. Hiding the fox under his cloak, the boy endures the agony of the fox gnawing at his entrails rather than confess the deed. Such a system created a warrior able to survive the cold and hunger of marches, to forage for himself, and to be wholly loyal to other Spartan fighters. Indeed, the entire society supported these martial values; even the women valued death with honor in battle for their sons. Famously, the Spartan mother in giving her son his shield for his first battle said to him: "Return with your shield or upon it."

At the age of twenty, the young man officially became a member of the Spartan army, living communally in barracks. He continued his military training, often practicing by killing helots, a custom that both maintained the subservience of the slaves that supported this warrior society and also inculcated a ruthlessness in killing those who were not Spartans.

Such a life intensified a warrior's affective bonds with fellow warriors rather than with family or women. In the *agoge*, at about the age of twelve, commonly the first stirrings of puberty, the Spartan boy formed a close relationship, often sexual, with an older youth. As with the samurai, the question of physical sex is less important than the method of employing the need for close emotional ties so strong at puberty as to intensify warrior loyalty. Such bonds knit together the fighting unit, encouraging courage and loyalty in battle. One is more likely to protect and even die for a person that one loves and to feel battle rage to avenge a lover who is killed. Achilles emerges from his tent to fight the Trojans only to avenge the death of Patroclus, his beloved companion.

Not until the age of thirty, having survived this extraordinarily rigorous training, was the Spartan male allowed to enter manhood as defined by Spartan mores. He then became a citizen. And as a citizen, he was required to marry. The strangeness, at least to us, of the Spartan marriage rites suggests the need within a warrior society to minimize heterosexual bonds while also breeding new generations of warriors. The classical historian Plutarch reports the peculiar practices of the Spartan wedding night:

> The custom was to capture women for marriage . . . The so-called "bridesmaid" took charge of the captured girl. She first shaved her head to the scalp, then dressed her in a man's cloak and sandals, and laid her down alone on a mattress in the dark. The bridegroom—who was not drunk and thus not impotent, but was sober as always—first had dinner in the messes, then would slip in, undo her belt, lift her and carry her to the bed.[9]

Such a unique custom suggests how even marriage was integrated into and served the functions of the warrior state. The female as a sexual object was transformed from female to male by losing her hair and being dressed in male clothing. The bridegroom continued to live in barracks with other men rather than establishing a family home; the woman was essentially raped as a soldier would, rather than courted. Strikingly, this arrangement of the husband living with other men or away fighting gave to the Spartan women more power than women in other classical societies. Rather than giving up the property she brought to marriage, she controlled her own resources; thus, a good portion of Spartan land lay in the hands of women.

Firm of body, trained from childhood in military skills, loyal to comrades and to the state rather than to family or wives, imbued with the warrior ethos of death before dishonor, and advancing in the phalanx in which each fighter protects the man next to him with his shield, the Spartan soldier was invincible in ground warfare against the armies of other Greek city-states. By the end of the fifth century BCE, Sparta had defeated Athens to become the ruling city-state of Greece. But only in the fourth century BCE did Spartan power, primarily because of the weakness of its navy, falter under the massive power of Persia.

Sparta's warrior culture lives on into our own time in the enduring story of the battle of Thermopylae, often called the battle of the Three Hundred. In the late fifth century BCE, an alliance of Greek city-states led by Sparta fought an invasion by the huge army of the Persian Empire lead by King Xerxes. In 480 BCE, Greeks sought to stop the Persians at the narrow pass of Thermopylae ("the hot gates") against a large Persian force. Here, protected by the narrow walls of the pass, the Greek phalanx could hold against the Persians. But the Persians found a mountain pass that allowed them to outflank the Greeks. Knowing they could not win, the Greeks retreated, but a contingent of 300 Spartans, led by King Leonidas, knowing they would die in the struggle, volunteered to hold the pass, thus allowing the retreat of the forces of other city-states. And die they did—fighting until their spears were broken, then with their short swords. The classical historian Herodotus relates: "Here they defended themselves to the last, those who still had swords using them, and the others resisting with their hands and teeth." Death before dishonor, indeed. A moving epitaph was then set in a monument at the site of the battle:

> Go tell the Spartans, thou who passest by,
> That here, obedient to their laws, we lie.

But what are we to make of the Spartan warrior state? Certainly Thermopylae has lasted into our own time in language and in highly popular films as the emblem of martial courage, of the sacrifice by free men for others, of seeking honor even to death. Sparta remains the ideal of warriors and those who aspire to be warriors. The Michigan State football team is called the Spartans. A book and a film about the sacrifices of soldiers in Vietnam are titled, in reference to the epitaph of Thermopylae, *Go Tell the Spartans*. The 2010 film *Restropo* documents life in an embattled, isolated outpost in a remote valley of Afghanistan. The elite American troops under fire each day have painted on a wall, in color, a Greek helmet with a horsehair crest and under that the word "Spartans" to honor their continuity with the warriors of Leonidas.

Yet for all our admiration of the Three Hundred who sacrificed their lives for their comrades and their state, the extreme case of Sparta shows the less positive side of the warrior ethos. There was in Sparta the prescribed guilt-free killing of helots, the slave class that supports the warriors, in order to shape a consciousness in which inferiors and men of other tribes can be killed without shame. *Agoge* creates a masculine identity that has no place for intellectuality and the arts; that eradicates any positive emotions for women and family; that sees heterosexual sex as useful only for the reproduction of strong fighting men; and that assumes a eugenics that validates killing males who are in any way physically unfit.

Nothing illustrates more forcefully the danger of the warrior ethos capturing an entire society than the attempt by the fascist movements of the mid-twentieth century to create a new society based on the Spartan warrior state. In Nazi Germany such an ideal was, for a time, realized and in Mussolini's fascist Italy only partly accomplished. The Nazi racial movement that sought to create strong and hard male bodies through the elimination of the deformed grew out of the contemporary eugenics movement. Like Sparta's cruel domination of the helots, Germany put into practice their ideology of scientific racism to treat what they saw as inferior races, such as the Slavs, as slaves to support the racially pure warrior *volk*. Like the Spartans, within a system of superiority, Germans were proud to show no shame: indeed a certain glory and honor resided in killing inferior races. The ideal German male in theory, if not in practice, was the warrior—hard of body and devoid of conscience—and powered not by the intellect but by the will and finding his highest moments in the explosion of violence. Within this extreme warrior ideal continuous with the Spartans, the Germans sought to create a New Man: the ideal warrior, the "man of steel." The fascist extremity of the warrior ideal is well articulated by the German writer Ernst Junger, a fascist who described the glory, even the ecstasy of fighting for his nation in World War I and looked forward to the emergence of a new identity for himself and for the nation through warfare, which he termed, in the title of his war novel *Storm of Steel:* "The Great Battle was a turning point for me . . . The incredible massing of forces in the hour of destiny, to fight for a distant future, and the violence."[10]

Although the Spartan ideal was for a time realized in the twentieth century as millions of those deemed inferior were killed, as Germans became devoted to glory and also to death, as the German armed forces performed as highly efficient fighting units, and the entire nation was focused on the glory of the Third Reich. Yet the Germans were defeated by the citizen-soldiers of the United States and its allies.

About Male Bonding

Intense bonds between men define warrior society. Loyalty to one's fellow warriors even to death is crucial. Men fight not for themselves but for their comrades. And revenge for one's fallen comrades is one of the primary spurs to battle rage.

To strengthen the emotional bonds between warriors, the affective bonds of men with women must be eliminated from experience and from consciousness. As boys, samurai and Spartans are taken from their families to live in communal all-male societies so that the warrior caste becomes his family. Later in life, heterosexual desire is subordinated to the chief virtue of the warrior: honor in the eyes of other men. The twentieth-century Japanese officer in Mishima's "Patriotism" engages in deeply satisfying sex with his wife before committing *seppuku* but kills himself nonetheless to honor Bushido. And we have noted how Spartan marriage rites are grounded not in courtship in which heterosexual affection grows, but in enacting the rape of a military campaign. The Greek warriors that camped outside Troy brought along women as slaves to be traded among men and used only for sexual purposes. Indeed, at the center of the narrative of the *Iliad*, Agamemnon, the king of the Greeks, takes Briseas, a slave girl that Achilles has won in battle, from Achilles. Achilles's celebrated rage at Agamemnon that leads him to sulk in his tent during battle is grounded not in affection for Briseas, but in the sense that his honor as a warrior entitled to his spoils has been violated by Agamemnon. Strikingly, we see that honor counts more than feelings for a woman and even for the satisfaction of heterosexual desire for a slave girl.

For warriors, intense affection is directed toward other men. The exemplary story of such erotically charged feeling among warriors is that between Achilles and Patroclus in the *Iliad*. Patroclus was adopted and brought up in the household of Achilles; the men considered themselves brothers: as parts of a single self. As Achilles stays in his tent because of the slight to his honor by Agamemnon, Patroclus dons Achilles's armor to fight. Hector, thinking that he is combating Achilles, kills Patroclus. The desire for revenge draws Achilles from his tent and triggers his battle rage as he confronts and kills Hector. Achilles and his men then prepare elaborate traditional mourning rites for Patroclus: burning the body on a pyre and searching through the ashes for bones to bury. For Achilles, his intense bond with Patroclus is more powerful than his allegiance to the cause of the Trojan War. It is personal revenge that brings him out to fight Hector, not the desire to conquer Troy or obey his king.

The question arises as to the extent to which this personal bond between warriors such as that of Achilles and Patroclus or of the samurai and the Spartans can be considered as sexual. But perhaps this is a misleading question. The question of whether or not they had sex, so central in our obsessive post-Freudian thinking, is less important than the universality of such deep emotional bonds among fighters. Bonds are functional in knitting together the fighting unit. They grow in the intimacy of men in battle and are intensified, as with Achilles, in the desire to avenge fallen comrades.

Discussion of this bond among warriors is clouded since we have no word in our language for this feeling. The word *bond* is too weak for the feeling of men in battle. Nor is the word *friendship* adequate. Clouded by the contemporary fear of homosexuality, we are reluctant to use the word *love* with its overtones of sexual physical attraction. But when the soldiers in the isolated outpost of Restropo dance with each other or wrestle partly nude, as did the Greek warriors at Patroclus's funeral rites, this cannot be seen as homosexuality but as a bond for which we have no name. The Greeks did have a term, *philia,* which refers to a variety of relationships: for example, to family, husband, and wife; but its general meaning is that of the strongest affective relation that a person can have, rather than specifically to bonds among men.[11] Perhaps the best terms we have for male affection in battle engage the terms *brother* and *brotherhood* in an analogy with the intensity and nonsexual nature of family feeling. A draftee in Vietnam observes: "It's a closeness you never had before. It's closer than your mother and fathers, closer than your brother or sister, or whoever you're closest with in your family. . . . We needed each other to survive."[12] The band of brothers is richly descriptive as the title of the popular book and TV series about a company of elite airborne troops in World War II.[13] The term band of brothers and the sense of fighting men as brothers refers to the most famous speech in English about the nobility of men joining together in battle. In Shakespeare's *Henry V,* in the most eloquent of battle speeches the king exhorts his troops on St Crispin's day before the battle of Agincourt against the seemingly overwhelming power of the French armored knights:

> And Crispin Crispian shall ne'er go by,
> From this day to the ending of the world,
> But we in it shall be remembered—
> We few, we happy few, we band of brothers;
> For he today that sheds his blood with me
> Shall be my brother.[14]

So the Marine Corps, our own warrior caste, emphasizes this bonding that goes beyond the rather pallid idea of cooperation: "*Semper Fidelis* distinguishes the Marine Corps bond from any other. It goes beyond team-work—it is a brotherhood that lasts for life."[15]

Going Berserk

Driven by revenge for his brother, Achilles flies into what can best be termed battle rage. Hector, too, casts off the restraints of civilization to become an animal, a bird of prey. He

> swooped like a soaring eagle
> launching down from the dark clouds to earth
> to snatch some helpless lamb or trembling hare.
> Achilles charged too, bursting with rage, barbaric.[16]

For warriors from Homer to the present day, the most highly valued and intense life moment comes when the self as conscious identity and ratio-nality disappears in a zone of pure instinct and the frenzy of killing more akin to the animal rather than the human. Each warrior society has a differ-ent name for this moment. From an ancient warrior society, the Norsemen, comes our term for battle rage: going berserk.

The Norsemen of Scandinavia, also known as the Vikings, a totalizing warrior society akin to the Spartans, conquered a large swath of Europe including England in the ninth and tenth centuries CE with their long-boats and swords. As their elite warriors, the Norse kings employed shock troops called berserkers. In battle, the berserkers underwent fits of what ap-peared at the time as a form of male madness that engendered superhuman strength, a temporary frenzy as reversion to uninhibited animality:

> This fury, which was called berserkergang, occurred not only in the heat of battle, but also during laborious work. Men who were thus seized performed things which otherwise seemed impossible for human power. This condition is said to have begun with shivering, chattering of the teeth, and chill in the body, and then the face swelled and changed its color. With this was con-nected a great hot-headedness, which at last gave over into a great rage, under which they howled as wild animals, bit the edge of their shields, and cut down everything they met without discriminating between friend or foe. When this condition ceased, a great dulling of the mind and feebleness followed, which could last for one or several days.[17]

For the samurai this loss of self in battle also entailed a purging of reason; but in contrast to *berserkergang,* this was, as we noted, a Zen state beyond thought that was free of animalistic rage. Following practices of Zen Buddhism and as in Zen archery, the mind had to be trained for "no mindedness" or the removal of distracting thought. Only after achieving this Zen state of concentration without distraction could striking with the sword be intuitive, free of thinking, and instantaneous with the rapidity enshrined now in popular samurai films. The end result of such concentration and practice was a samurai's ability to draw his sword and kill an enemy in one smooth movement. A modern analogy would be with the commonly experienced "zone" in sports in which time slows down and action is intuitive. A football quarterback—a current equivalent of the warrior—has only a few seconds to see the entire field and almost instantaneously decides to throw the pass or to run.

Within the militaristic fascist societies of modern times, this amoral joy in killing became the supreme value as casting off the constraints of middle-class bourgeois life for the authentic primal manliness. Here is Junger describing that moment in World War I that he experienced and longed to make the center of emotional life for those in Nazi Germany. Like the American General Patton of World War II, Junger feels his authentic identity as the reincarnation of ancient warriors. Charging the enemy lines with his brothers, he channels the rage of the berserkers:

> Our rage broke like a storm. Thousands must have fallen already. That was clear; and even though the shelling continued, it felt quiet, as though it had lost its imperative thrust.
>
> As we advanced, we were in the grip of a berserk rage. The overwhelming desire to kill lent wings to my stride. Rage squeezed bitter tears from my eyes. The immense desire to destroy that overhung the battlefield precipitated a red mist in our brains. We called our sobbing and stammering fragments of sentences to one another, and an impartial observer might have concluded that we were all ecstatically happy.[18]

Such instances of battle rage are pervasive in combat spurred by the need to overcome moral inhibitions and by the desire to avenge brothers fallen in battle, as in the celebrated rage of Achilles. Such moments came to drafted American soldiers in Vietnam, although tinged with remorse afterward as the soldier returned to life in a democracy. Here is an example as described by an American veteran of Vietnam—of becoming, like Achilles and Hector under the brutal conditions of war, an animal and another person:

> I was [an] . . . animal. When I look back at that stuff, I say, "That was somebody else that did that. Wasn't me. That wasn't me." Y'know, "Who the . . . was that?" y'know, at the time it didn't mean nothing. It didn't change nothing.

> War change you, changes you. Strips you, strips you of all your beliefs, your religion, takes your dignity away, you become an animal. I know that animals don't. . . . Y'know, it's unbelievable what humans do to each other.[19]

The berserk state with its accession of physical power, sense of personal invulnerability, lessening of the social taboos against killing, and loss of the controls of social life is invaluable to the survival and power of men in combat. And yet this explosive rage and violence that lies at the heart of warrior identity poses enormous problems for the warrior himself and for his society. For any society needs to maintain order when battle is over; the violent warrior must be controlled when peace comes. That the berserker in his frenzy could kill friend as well as foe posed an obvious problem, and the berserkers were gradually phased out by the Norse kings.

And for the warrior himself, the coming of the berserk state can violate his self-identity as warrior. For the loss of consciousness and of the inhibitions of civilized morality can lead the fighter to violate the code of honor that is crucial to his being. On the plains of Troy as in the jungles of Vietnam, men in *berserkergang* commit atrocities. The American soldier in Vietnam quoted above confesses: "I became a . . . ing animal. I started . . . ing putting . . . ing heads on poles. Digging up . . . ing graves. I didn't give a . . . anymore."[20] In the classic epic of war, after killing Hector, Achilles's berserker state does not pass. Instead, his rage for revenges compels him to contravene the warrior ethos of respect for the enemy warrior by mutilating Hector's body, dragging it behind his chariot, and refusing at first the usual custom of returning to his comrades the dead body of the warrior.

Men cannot live in battle rage. It must pass, and they must return to live within a society at peace. The berserker rage of Achilles must be exorcised. In a particularly moving section of the *Iliad,* Hector's aged father, Priam, comes to Achilles's camp to plead for the return of the body of his son. The epic ends as Achilles, now feeling after battle the return of human sympathy and the need to return to obedience to codes of honor, restores the body to Priam. That the gods have miraculously restored the body after its mutilation by Achilles suggests the divine imperative for purging the frenzy of battle rage.

The debilitating "great dulling of the mind and feebleness" felt by the berserkers after the fit of battle passes bears close similarity to the feelings experienced by veterans of Vietnam and Iraq, especially to the psychic numbing: the inability to feel that is one of the major elements of what is now termed posttraumatic stress disorder (PTSD). The veteran seeks to forget or suppress the animalistic violence and loss of comrades in battle.

For the Norse berserker, the weakness will pass, and he will return to battle; his primary identity as warrior continues. For the American veteran, this numbness derives from the psychological effort needed to purge the self of battle rage in order to return to civilian life. The explosions of violence by veterans against family and society indicate the continuing problem of how to return to civilian life by the soldiers who experience this frenzy in war. The draftees that fought in Vietnam had a split masculine identity: they were asked to become warriors for a time, even berserkers in the jungles of Vietnam—then asked at enormous personal cost to cast off that identity and put on the contrasting masculine identity of restrained, married, hard-working male citizens.[21]

The Warrior in Contemporary America

From its inception, the United States has been distrustful of warriors and of warrior castes. Looking to the example of Europe, the founding fathers feared that the warrior ethos might override the principles of the new American democracy. The founders, many of whom were citizen-soldiers themselves, sought to establish a republic with a citizen-army. Civilian control of the military is a cardinal principle of constitutional rule with the elected president the commander in chief of the armed forces.

Rather than warriors whose lives are wholly devoted to battle, American military heroes are citizens who perform the role of soldier when called, as in democratic Athens, then return to their primary masculine identities as farmers or merchants or politicians. The revered icons of American life are such citizen-soldiers—the Minutemen of Lexington and Concord who left their farms, muskets in hand, to repel the British Redcoats. Their monument standing at the bridge in Concord, Massachusetts, where the first skirmish of the Revolutionary War took place carries the words of Ralph Waldo Emerson's "Hymn," sung at the completion of it in 1836. His justly celebrated words praise the American ideal of the citizen who lays down his plow to pick up his musket:

> By the rude bridge that arched the flood,
> Their flag to April's breeze unfurled,
> Here once the embattled farmers stood,
> And fired the shot heard round the world.[22]

The commander of the Revolutionary War armies, George Washington, beautifully stated, "When we assumed the soldier, we did not lay aside the citizen."[23] After leading the new nation to independence and serving as president, he returned to his life as a prosperous farmer. American films of World War II celebrate the ethnically mixed platoons whose members are reluctantly drafted but bravely fight the Germans or the Japanese and long to return to their families and girlfriends and jobs at home. The American military academies—West Point and Annapolis—take candidates recommended by members of Congress, thus preventing the growth of a hereditary warrior class. The draft conscripting all men to fight in times of crisis, such as World War I, World War II, and the Korean and Vietnam wars, was devoted to the existence of a citizen-army rather than an army of full-time warriors.

The citizen-army in America generated a split in masculine identity. A draftee from a democratic society unused to taking orders, with an internalized taboo against killing, and whose primary affective life is heterosexual is forced with great psychic difficulty to learn the drill and to kill, to become part of a war machine. As such, the conscripted soldier differs from the full-time warrior whose very being is that of a killer/fighter. Draftees just want to go home. In Vietnam, the draftee—a soldier, often against his will—was flown quickly home after serving exactly 365 days. For non-professional American soldiers in Vietnam, the commitment to honor and loyalty and to country evaporated as they came to see the fighting as meaningless and often turned against their commanders.

The split identity between the self as citizen and the self as warrior is the stuff of American war writing and war films. In World War II films, the guy from Brooklyn and the guy from the farm in the Midwest are reluctant to fight, but combat evokes a battle rage against the Germans and the Japanese. Tim O'Brien, a veteran of Vietnam, writes brilliantly of fighting not as an expression of a primal identity as warrior but for the draftee as a performance, a self-conscious role of soldier played for other men: "They carried their reputations. They carried the soldier's greatest fear, which is the fear of blushing. Men killed, and died, because they were embarrassed not to. It was what had brought them to the war in the first place, nothing positive, no dreams of glory or honor, just to avoid the blush of dishonor. They died so as not to die of embarrassment."[24]

Most nations, at times, need to wage war. In the aftermath of the deep political conflicts about the Vietnam War fought mainly by draftees, in a major shift the traditional American ideal of the citizen-army filled by conscription was replaced with an all-volunteer armed force of full-time professional soldiers. This volunteer army incorporates elite forces that self-consciously live by the ancient warrior ethos—the SEALS; the Green Berets; the Rangers; other Special Operations forces; and, of long standing, the Marine Corps.

The Marine Corps has self-consciously fashioned its identity as a warrior caste. A man is not forced to be but chooses to be a Marine. As with the samurai and the Spartan, being a Marine is a way of being. A man does not merely join the Corps; he *becomes* a Marine. A draftee or even a volunteer soldier on leaving another service may think of himself an ex-sailor or an ex-soldier as he puts off his fighting identity to resume his life as a middle-class family man. But one cannot be an "ex-Marine." "Once a Marine, always a Marine" is a proud motto of the Corps. A man *is* a Marine even after leaving active service. This is his core identity, and it cannot be changed. Being a Marine is a totalizing life-long identity. Like a true warrior, he does not yearn to go to his domestic home; the Marine Corps is his spiritual home.

The Marines quite self-consciously figure themselves as continuing the ancient warrior tradition. Their central virtues are those of the warrior ethos: "Honor, Courage, Commitment." For all the American tradition of a citizen-army, the Corps sees itself as a distinct self-perpetuating warrior caste. The anachronistic sword worn by all officers and noncommissioned officers is "more than a weapon, a heritage," a symbol recalling battles of the Marines as far back as ridding the Mediterranean in the 1820s of pirates on the "shores of Tripoli," a campaign remembered in the Marine Corps hymn. Recruits are told: "You have the courage to stand on an impenetrable line of warriors stretching back 234 years."[25] The "impenetrable line of warriors" refers beyond American history to the impenetrable phalanx of the Spartans at Thermopylae. As the berserkers were the shock troops of the Norse kings, the Marines are the elite forces of the American armed services. Their own recruiting motto figures them as an elite—"The few, the proud, the Marines."

The well-known motto of the Corps is "*Semper Fidelis,*" "always faithful." It means being faithful to the nation, certainly, but also faithful to the Corps and to one's fellow Marines. The official recruiting manifesto asks the potential recruit for his "commitment to stand shoulder to shoulder." At the core of this contemporary American warrior elite is the intense male-male bond of warriors. Like the Greeks and the Trojans of the *Iliad,* a Marine does not leave the body of a fallen comrade behind. This is a bond between men for which, as we have seen, we do not have an adequate name; our closest term is brotherhood. And for its unifying emotional principle, the Corps turns also to this term. As noted, the official words of the Corps express warrior loyalty: "*Semper Fidelis* distinguishes the Marine Corps bond from any other. It goes beyond teamwork—it is a brotherhood that lasts for life."[26]

The inclusion of such volunteer fighting units has intensified the American ambivalence about the place of a warrior caste in a democratic society. Conflict arises in that, as we have seen, the warrior code sets as the highest value personal honor and loyalty to brother warriors, while the American ideal of civilian control of the military sees the primary allegiance of the soldier as loyalty to the president as commander-in-chief as stated in the Constitution. Furthermore, the volunteer soldier is a professional in that his primary role is fulfilling his mission as ordered. Unlike a draftee, he does not bring the civilian values of a civilian identity to his time in the service. Thus, the internal conflicts of the citizen-soldier questioning the values and purpose of the mission, seen so starkly in the near mutinies of the Vietnam conflict, do not appear. The professional soldier ideally does his job without questioning its purpose.

The American problem of reconciling allegiance to civilian authority with the code of the warrior necessitates the oaths that the new volunteer soldier must swear. The professional soldier must take the Oath of Enlistment required of all U.S. service personnel. Here, obedience to the U.S. Constitution is placed first and foremost: "I do solemnly swear (or affirm) that I will support and defend the Constitution of the United States against all enemies, foreign and domestic; that I will bear true faith and allegiance to the same; and that I will obey the orders of the President of the United States and the orders of the officers appointed over me."

The soldier must then swear to the Soldier's Creed. Although this creed in no way supersedes the Oath of Enlistment, it does indicate the explicit and somewhat controversial effort to transform all soldiers, not only the elite units such as the Marine Corps, into warriors modeled on the ancient warrior ethos:

> I am an American Soldier.
> I am a Warrior and a member of a team.
> I serve the people of the United States, and live the Army Values.
> I will always place the mission first.
> I will never accept defeat.
> I will never quit.
> I will never leave a fallen comrade.
> I am disciplined, physically and mentally tough, trained and proficient in my warrior tasks and drills.

I always maintain my arms, my equipment and myself.
I am an expert and I am a professional.
I stand ready to deploy, engage, and destroy, the enemies of the United States
of America in close combat.

This creed exhibits the contradictions about the position of the warrior in contemporary American life, especially in the sections referring to the warrior ethos.

I will always place the mission first.
I will never accept defeat.
I will never quit.
I will never leave a fallen comrade.[27]

These ideals, especially in the sense that "I will always place the mission first," as consistent as they may be with the warrior code seem to contradict the ideal of the citizen-soldier as placing obedience to the president and Constitution first. Here the mission seems to take precedence over national values that are the goal of warfare. And the primary loyalties for the American professional soldiers, for the Marines as well as the Spartans and Trojans, are to military brotherhood: "I will never leave a fallen comrade." And the skill of "close combat" is more appropriate to the warriors on the plains of Troy than to a high-tech army.

With the abolition of the draft, the experience of actual combat with its intensity and its suffering has become further and further removed from the lives of ordinary American men. With the universal draft of World War II, Korea, and Vietnam increasingly a memory, only a few professional soldiers experience war. But the elements of the warrior ethos—bravery, physical courage, brotherhood, honor, loyalty to other men, losing oneself in the rage of combat—remain attractive to males even as participation in war lived by this ethos drifts further and further away from lives of men in corporate America. Paradoxically, the less that American men are called to assume the warrior identity with its threat of actual harm, the more these warrior qualities have informed popular culture to be experienced vicariously without the threat of bodily pain and death. The warrior battle ethos is practiced for most men only in the imagination. The ethos or code is admired from afar, not as part of a man's bodily life.

Films about warriors real and imagined remain increasingly popular. The movie *Patton* was and remains highly popular as the story of a warrior leading armies yet psychologically removed from the citizen-army he led.

Documentaries about World War II in Europe and the Pacific run ceaselessly on TV. The warriors of other cultures in their idealized Hollywood versions fill the imagination as cartoon samurai, or ninjas, or the Spartan 300 who sacrificed themselves at Thermopylae. Even the Mafia, as idealized in the *Godfather* films, is admired for its code of honor, its brutality in killing for the family, and its adherence to a code.

For American adult men, the transmutation of warrior identity from actual bloody fighting and killing to vicarious experience takes place primarily through sports. Teams named the Warriors or the Spartans abound. The enormous popularity of professional football for men who spend their weekdays before computer screens lies in its distanced reenactment of the combat and code of the *Iliad*. Pro football is limned in metaphors of war: the quarterback throws a "bomb"; games are enlivened by "hits." The morals of hegemonic masculinity are suspended as men play through pain with rare physical courage, breaking the body to achieve victory and honor. The entire game is an extended *berserkergang* as linemen lose their sense of self-preservation in battle rage as they hit the enemy linemen. Men of extraordinary bodily strength and martial skill move to their mission and care for fallen comrades.

In the National Football conference championship game in which the veteran quarterback Brett Favre suffered a number of "vicious hits," he played on. After the game loss, as he taped up his ankle that was "as purple as his uniform" he said, "It was a physical game. A lot of hits, but if you win, then you sure feel a lot better." With the comradeship of warriors, even of enemy warriors, the victorious quarterback Drew Brees praised Favre for following the warrior code. Honor was still more important than victory: "He battled. . . . He's a warrior. He always has been."[28]

Chapter 2

Athens and the Emergence of Democratic Man

As Sparta was shaping a society of warriors, in the fourth and fifth centuries BCE in Athens, another city-state of the Greek peninsula, a new and extraordinarily influential form of government arose—participatory democracy, government by the people rather than by autocratic kings. Rule was by the will of the people or *demos* through elections, debate in public meetings, and government administration by the ordinary citizen. The exemplary man was now defined as the citizen, an identity that continues into our own time. In the words of Werner Jaeger, the foremost scholar of Athenian culture, the citizen was a "new type of man" being shaped by, and also shaping, the city of Athens.[1] Athens rejected the often brutal virility of the warrior and the extravagance of kings for a manliness grounded in moderation; intellectual cultivation; social responsibility; and martial courage, as well as physical beauty. As stated by Pericles, the statesman and general who in large part created "the golden age" of Athens of the fifth century BCE: "Our city is worthy of admiration. We cultivate refinement without extravagance and knowledge without effeminacy."[2]

The Athenian citizen was a member of an exclusive group within a deeply patriarchal society. The legal status of citizen was granted only to males over the age of eighteen who had been born there as the children of citizens. Limited, then, to free-born males, the identity of citizen excluded much of the population of Athens. Free-born women could not be citizens. The tradesmen and craftsmen who crowded Athens from other cities were excluded, as were the multitude of slaves who served the citizens and performed much of the manual labor. Indeed, the identity of citizen was defined as the opposite of the slave. Personal freedom as freedom from the rule of tyrants and freedom of the individual self in distinction to the merging of the individual into the mass army as in Sparta remained the foundation of Athenian manliness.

If in the Homeric world and in Sparta, the primary identity of man was as warrior, for democratic Athens, fighting in the infantry phalanx or manning the galleys of the Athenian Navy in times of military exigency was indeed the duty of a citizen; but in contrast to the Spartan man, it was only one of the many duties and responsibilities of the Athenian citizen. Instead, for the citizen of Athens, masculine identity consisted of performing responsibly in a number of areas: performing military service for the city-state, administering the democratic society, and fulfilling the responsibilities of head of household. It was his demonstration of intelligence and trustworthiness in carrying out these obligations that made him a man. As Pericles stated, "I doubt if the world can produce a man who, where he has only himself to depend upon, is equal to so many emergencies, and graced by so happy a versatility, as the Athenian."[3]

To perform these demanding and multiple tasks demanded an array of skills. To participate in the open forums of direct democracy called for training in eloquence and learning the rhetoric of persuasion. To work in the administration of the government and in the deliberations of juries in the open courts called for a flexibility of mind. For all the tasks of peacetime, the Athenians sought a philosophic mind created through what we now call a liberal education, one of the major contributions of Athens to Western culture. Following the warrior ethos in universal military service demanded a sound and sturdy body trained in the arts of war.

For the Athenian citizen, then, honor in life and reputation after death were not limited to valor in battle. Honor for the citizen of a democracy lay in performing the diverse roles of politician, soldier, and head of household with the qualities that defined Athenian manliness—a sense of responsibility, moderation, and good judgment. Furthermore, as we shall see, these public activities were informed by a strong homosocial unity with other citizens and grounded in the homoerotic relations between adult citizens and adolescent boys about to become citizens.

Maintaining manliness is a life's work for a man. A man may be born an Athenian citizen, but performance of manliness in accord with Athenian standards was a ceaseless occupation. Within the multiple sites of manly duty for the Athenian citizen, the primary motivating force was maintaining personal honor and reputation. In Athens, maintaining a good name provided the motivating energy for the citizen. As in the warrior societies of Sparta and feudal Japan, Athens was a shame society. A man avoided shame by performing his duties as citizen of a democracy. A man's worth was validated by visible actions in the public and domestic spheres and on the battlefield. Manliness was located not deep in the soul nor regulated by internalized guilt, but manifested in public performance judged by fellow citizens. For the Athenian citizen, the sense of self flourished by following his society's code of manly behavior. As Pericles states in his "Funeral Oration," men live by "that code which, although unwritten, yet cannot be broken without acknowledging disgrace."[4]

This first democracy, then, generated the ideal of man as citizen. In the more than two thousand years since the establishment of Athenian democracy, this ideal form of democratic manhood—a belief in duty to the state, the developed mind, intellectual suppleness, the oratorical ability to persuade fellow citizens in counsel, and physical courage in battle—has provided a model, as the lives of our own American founding fathers testify, for the identity of man in a democratic society.

Manliness as Public Service in a Participant Democracy

The system of government we call democracy was invented in the city-state of Athens and flourished there in the fourth and fifth centuries BCE. Unlike American democracy, Athenian democracy was a radically participatory system: a direct rather than representative structure. Gathered in the Assembly, all citizens, rather than their elected officials, gathered to pass laws, decide to wage war, approve treaties, appoint or dismiss military commanders, and pass on the allocation of the wealth and resources of the city-state. Within the small population of the city-state, all citizens—that is, all free-born males—were granted equal rights; and in return, all citizens were required to participate in the administration of the polity and in juries of the courts of law.

The Assembly (*demos*) was the central institution of Athenian democracy. Consisting of all citizens, the Assembly met in an outdoor amphitheater on a hillside of the city with a usual attendance of about 6,000 citizens. The Assembly voted usually by a show of hands on laws brought to its attention by the Council, a smaller governing body, and other matters brought to its attention by its citizens. Here all citizens were entitled to speak to the gathering; none, not even the citizen craftsman or tradesman, were excluded. This right to speak is a vivid example of the freedom of the Athenian citizen. Although some citizens were known for their oratorical skill and spoke more frequently, within this egalitarian political site to gain reputation as a leader depended not on aristocratic birth, but primarily on the ability to speak persuasively and in a compelling fashion in the forum of citizens. Thus, training in the art of rhetoric became a necessary and valued element in the education of a citizen looking to attain leadership in the community. And compelling oratorical performance in the Assembly of one's equals became one marker of Athenian manliness.

In this participatory democracy, it was assumed that all citizens were able to perform the administrative responsibilities of government. Quite remarkably to us, positions of governmental administration were chosen by lot. This was a polity controlled neither by professional politicians nor long-term bureaucratic specialists. For example, the city-state had the Council consisting of 500 members that provided full-time government administration and agenda items for the Assembly. For all its importance, the Council was selected by a lottery. To prevent the entrenchment of power, the terms were for only one year. For the Athenian citizen, public service was a normal part of life as a man. And this was a manly duty to be carried out in public, not for private gain, but with honesty, responsibility, skill, and concern for the community.

For all citizens, the most direct participation in maintaining the state came in the deciding of legal cases in the People's Court. Here, men were chosen randomly from a pool of people willing to serve on large jury panels ranging from 500–1,500, depending on the importance of the case. And here, citizens functioning as what we would call jurors decided both criminal and civil legal disputes and determined punishment. All citizens were eligible, with payment provided, as in the American system, so that even the poorer citizens could serve. It should be noted that functions in the Court were not given to elected officials nor limited, as in our society, to certified professionals. There were neither lawyers nor judges in the trials. Defendants usually pleaded their own cases without written texts, calling on memorization and improvisation in the questioning. This participatory justice system in which all men were treated equally assumed oratorical ability, intellectual skill, and good judgment in the citizen as the components of Athenian masculinity. Such civic ideals of manliness continue into our own democratic jury system, which although administered by judges and lawyers, still depends on the participation of all citizens, both male and female, and on the assumption of good judgment and respect for political fairness as the mark of the citizen.

In the political life of Athens, then, the citizen inhabits both an individual and a collective identity. The citizen derives his sense of self as a free person participating in the collective life of the city-state in accord with the ideals of Athenian manliness. He makes personal judgments to shape the will of the *demos* in deciding the fate of the city in war and peace. Not to participate as an individual in these collective duties would be to invite the social shame placed upon a man who did not fulfill his manly responsibilities. In his "Funeral Oration," a panegyric to the virtues of Athenian manhood, Pericles praised the uniqueness of his city: "Our ordinary citizens, though occupied with the pursuits of industry, are still fair judges of public matters ... instead of looking on discussion as a stumbling-block in the way of action, we think it an indispensable preliminary to any wise action at all."[5]

Education: A Sound Mind in a Sound Body

To achieve success in these varied duties of manhood, the Athenians invented and practiced a new form of education, the origin of what we call a liberal education that continues as an ideal into our own time. If the Spartan system of *agoge* shaped men for a warrior identity of simple obedience, for the loss of self in the military unit and even for the eradication of thought itself, the Athenian system of education aimed to creating a quality of mind termed *paideia,* the fully developed, well-rounded, intellectually supple self that suits men to take their place in a democratic society. This intellectual quality, *paideia,* became the marker of Athenian manliness.[6]

The education to form citizens began early. The male children of citizens voluntarily attended school from about the age of seven until the age of fourteen. Here they learned writing and reading, primarily from the Homeric epics thought to be a source of moral value. It must be noted, however, that although all citizens were allowed and indeed expected to participate in governing, there was still a class system within education. In a way that resonates with our own class divisions in schooling, for the *banausoi,* a distinct group of craftsmen that included sculptors as well as nail makers, tanners, architects, and other craftsmen, there existed what we now call vocational education, a narrower and more focused training in craft.[7]

At the age of fourteen, those who could afford private tuition continued their education, while the less wealthy took an apprenticeship in the craft or trade. For the wealthy and well-connected elite citizen, such as Pericles, destined for positions of responsibility in the democracy, there existed the full liberal education grounded in the ideal of *paideia.* There were no institutions like our universities, but young men of wealth until the age of eighteen associated themselves with private tutors to study the abstractions of philosophy, both as a training for leadership and as an end in itself. Plato and Aristotle had their own school for young men. As Plato's dialogues indicate, his mission of teaching as expanding the sensibility of other men continued in formal and informal ways through his life, as through the lives of elite citizens.

In contrast to Sparta, the schooling of the citizen looked to shape an enriched sensibility, one of the highest virtues of Athenian manliness. The curriculum included music, particularly learning to play the lyre; and singing, since that was thought to develop a sense of inner harmony. At a young age, boys learned the rules of correct expression that formed the basis for the study and practice of rhetoric or persuasive speech as adults. For leaders of the democratic state, oratory as the power to speak persuasively in the Assembly of the *polis* and in the courts was another skill of manhood.

The Athenians firmly believed that for true manliness, the philosophic activity of the mind was intertwined with the healthy activity of the body. They saw a profound fusion of the spiritual with the physical in the male body, a fullness of the male self that has been lost to us as we have split intellectual from athletic prowess. This Athenian ideal of manliness lingers vestigially in the ideal of the scholar-athlete that some universities support rhetorically even in the face of the increasing professionalization of college athletics. Young Athenians were expected to train their bodies. After school they would go to the *palaestra,* an outdoor space devoted to practice in such physical activities as wrestling, swimming, running, and throwing the discus: sports that continue in our modern Olympic Games. The goals of such devotion to the body were several. As we shall see, Athenian education trained men for warfare. But what we would call a buff body marked a good in itself for the Athenians. The ideal Athenian man lived in a beautiful body.

Classical Greek sculpture gave material form to this ideal of male beauty, as in the celebrated statue of the *Discus Thrower* or *Discobolus.*[8] In his classic study *The Nude,* Kenneth Clark sees the work as a supreme example of artistic skill in its figuring in sculptural form of the Athenian masculine ideal in its harmony and balance, its energy fused with self-control, and all suffused by intellect: "By sheer intelligence, Myron has created the enduring pattern of athletic energy ... The body, tense as a drawn bow, is, in its totality, like some Euclidean diagram of energy; and within this main figure the disposition of the parts has a clarity and a logic. ... A violent emphasis or a sudden acceleration of rhythmic movement would have destroyed those qualities of balance and completeness."[9]

Discus throwing was an important event in the Greek Olympic Games held every four years as the city-states of Greece put aside their continuous warfare to gather for the competition at the sacred site of Mount Olympus. An indication of the fullness of Greek culture, the Games included competitions for artists, sculptors, and poets as well as for athletes. But the focus was on the athlete. Not only Athens but also the other Greek city-states treasured athletic skill and saw the trained male body as the sign of true manliness and even as partaking of the divine. The young men competed nude under the admiring eyes of the male spectators in a range of events. Throwing the discus was one element in the pentathlon, a set of five events including the long jump, javelin throw, a short foot race, and wrestling. There was also boxing using hard leather gloves weighted with metal.

The Olympic Games since their revival in 1896 have continued many of the classical events. In a deeper way, the modern games sought to restore the Athenian ideal of manliness in the emphasis that was termed the amateur ideal. That the athletes had to be amateurs was a way of continuing the sense that athletic skill was the attribute of all citizens, rather than of narrowly trained professionals. Olympic victors in the ancient world were honored by their cities with commemorative statues. The amateur ideal continued the Athenian sense that a citizen would be shamed by taking money for performing his expected duty.

Citizen as Warrior

The final event of the ancient Olympic Games was the hoplite run in which young men raced wearing their battle armor. The inclusion of this event as well as wrestling, boxing, and the javelin throw indicates that the Greek training of young men to an ideal of physical grace and stamina had not only the sensual purpose of exhibiting male beauty, but also the functional purpose of preparing men for warfare on behalf of the city-state.

Athens depended upon its citizen-army. The development of courage and martial manliness was seen not as innate, but as needing nurturing and development by social institutions. At the ages of eighteen and nineteen, Athenian youths, *ephebes*, joined the military training institution called the *ephebeia*. This compulsory organization instilled in the young men military skills needed for the defense of the state, such as use of the hoplite spear and shield needed in the phalanx. Combat in the Athenian phalanx demanded the warrior values of courage, loyalty to comrades, and particularly self-control so as to maintain the formation. Furthermore, the phalanx constituted a form of warfare suitable for a democracy. The phalanx transferred the role of the warrior from the aristocracy to the people for the phalanx depended not on the prowess of a single hero such as Achilles, but on the cooperation and responsibility of the citizen-fighters as hoplites. Thus, training Athenian youth to be hoplite warriors became an important task, though not the sole one, of educating young men in their identity as citizens. Besides learning specific martial skills, the regimentation of the *ephebeia* with its communal life, training in obedience, and the forging of a sense of duty created at this impressionable age an internalized social identity as being part of a communal state with the necessity of following out one's duty to that state.[10]

In their time within the military sphere, the warrior ethos prevailed, even if it did not carry over into other masculine roles. Strikingly, the Athenians who prided themselves on their fully developed mind in civilian life drew their martial ideals from the tribal codes of the Homeric epics that were required reading within the schools. Drawn from the hierarchical rather than democratic Homeric world, the warrior code—death before dishonor, loyalty to comrades, and courage on the battlefield—prevailed in this compulsory military service. Manliness for the citizen in war was judged by his performance in battle. As Pericles said at the funeral of those Athenian citizens who died in the war against Sparta, "In the business before them, they thought fit to act boldly and trust in themselves. Thus choosing to die resisting, rather than to live submitting, they fled only from dishonor, but met danger face to face."[11]

Yet the Athenians saw in their own unique democratic system the source of their military prowess. In his "Funeral Oration," Pericles compares the individual freedom of the Athenian citizen's life to the harsh martial education (*agoge*), the "painful discipline" of the Spartans. He sees this openness of democratic life in contrast to a strict martial training as creating a more patriotic and more powerful fighting force:

> While in education, where our rivals from their very cradles by a painful discipline seek after manliness, at Athens we live exactly as we please, and yet are just as ready to encounter every legitimate danger. In proof of this it may be noticed that the Lacedaemonians [Spartans] do not invade our country alone, but bring with them all their confederates; while we Athenians advance unsupported into the territory of a neighbor, and fighting upon a foreign soil usually vanquish with ease men who are defending their homes.[12]

As Joseph Roisman, a scholar of Athenian masculinity, summarizes:

Despite the changing realities of war in the fourth century, Athenian public discourse held on tenaciously to archaic (or archaizing) values and per-
ceptions of military service. The hoplitic ethos, which highlighted honor,
cooperation, disciplined obedience, solidarity, patriotism, and striving for
excellence, as well as the attainment of victory in a well-regulated, open, and
face-to-face confrontation between nonprofessional soldiers, underpinned
the image of the ideal military figure, whether simply soldier or general, but
also that of the desirable citizen and man.[13]

In general, then, the performance of men in war became a prime, but not
the sole marker, of their manliness. A failure to serve, what we would call
draft dodging, or cowardice on the battlefield was taken as a mark of dishonor and signified a loss of manliness. This equation of responsible military service with manliness applied to all citizens. Even Socrates served as a
hoplite. In *The Symposium*, Alcibiades's praise of Socrates for his virtues of
bravery and loyalty to comrades on the battlefield shows that following the
warrior code was expected of even the loftiest of philosophers:

During the battle after which the generals awarded me the prize for bravery,
it was Socrates, no one else, who rescued me. He wasn't prepared to leave me
when I was wounded and so he saved my life as well as my armour and weapons. I actually told the general to award the prize for bravery on that occasion
to you, Socrates.

What struck me was how self-possessed he was . . . he was calmly looking out
both for friends and enemies, and it was obvious to everyone even from a long
distance that if anyone tackled this man, he would put up a tough resistance.[14]

And yet, it must be emphasized, for all of the manly honor accruing to
the display of courage in battle, the primary Athenian masculine identity
was not that of a warrior or the model of the samurai or of the berserker.
As the exemplary figure of Socrates as represented by Plato demonstrates,
martial valor and hoplitic hardiness were but one component of Athenian
manly identity. For, of course, Socrates was also a philosopher, educating
the young as well as the old, in the values of reason and moderation.

Manliness in the Erotic Life of the Citizen

The erotic life of the Athenian citizen cannot easily be represented in our
own rather reductive categories of gay/straight or heterosexual/ homosexual

(see chapter 7). For the Athenian citizen, manliness was not identified with a virility expressed in often predatory sexual relations with women. Nor, again in contrast to our predominant paradigms, was unmanliness linked to same-sex sexual desire and practice. For the Athenians, sexual relations with adolescent boys as well as with women were accepted as natural, pleasurable, and beautiful. Rather than defining manliness by the object of sexual desire: that is, by attraction to the opposite sex or the same sex, manliness in regard to sexuality was defined as the application of the values of the Athenians to the working out of natural sexual desire with moderation and self-control. In keeping with the Athenian ideal of male individuality and freedom, manly men must assure that in sexual activity with boys, neither partner is rendered subservient nor dominated by the other. In keeping with the Athenian disdain of trade, sexual acts with other males must not be governed by the exchange of money.

As we have seen, in warrior societies such as Sparta and feudal Japan, boys were guided into manhood through intense relations with older men that often included physical sexuality. The Athenians too evolved a system of mentoring the future citizen through close emotional and sexual bonds between the adolescent (*erastes*) and the adult citizen (*eromenos*). Adult citizens, usually elite ones, would form an erotic attachment to a physically beautiful youth, most often an adolescent at the moment of transition between boyhood and manhood, and most generally between the ages of fifteen to seventeen. For the Athenian erotic imagination, the youth at this moment represented the epitome of male beauty. This phase of man-boy erotics was crucial in the development of the citizen to be and of the state by forging the homosocial bonds that united the democracy.

With its homoerotic energy, this pervasive relation of adult citizens with adolescents by its nature generated a tension between Eros and honor, between fulfilling desire and maintaining manly control of the self. Desire always poses a threat to reason, that mark of Athenian manliness, and the possibility of subverting duty to the household and to the state. Thus the society developed an unwritten code of manly behavior to control erotic desire. The Athenian erotic most closely resembles what we would now call courtship, with an emphasis on negotiating power relations. The adolescent (*erastes*) had his power over the adult male (*eromenos*) that emerged from his desirability; the *eromenos* had a power that came of his adult position. The elaborate courtship followed rules that negotiated such dynamics. For example, the boy as prospective citizen would be shamed for selling his sexual favors and even denied the status of citizen. The adult could not use force. The Athenian man-boy relation became a kind of dance as each maintained the code of manliness.

We can see this relation as a coming-of-age rite in which a young man is tested before being initiated into manhood. As mentoring, the courtship employed sexual passion on both sides to guide the youth to democratic manhood. Such liaisons were generally accepted and highly valued. Plato's *Symposium* suggests the fusion of sexual desire with civic function: "The lover must be able to develop the boyfriend's understanding and virtue in general, and the boyfriend must want to acquire education and wisdom in general. When all these conditions are met, then and then alone it is right for a boyfriend to gratify his lover, but not otherwise."[15]

For the Athenians, then, man-boy relations were consistent with manliness, but only if the relation adhered to the unwritten rules. The abhorrence with which we reject such man-boy relations as pederasty simply did not exist. Same-sex male desire was not equated with unmanliness for the Athenians. When the boy became an adult and citizen, he would continue his relation with his *eromenos* but usually in a nonsexual form. Same-sex relations between adult citizens were rare and considered beyond the norm since such relations would mean that one of the adult citizens would be penetrated and thus become subservient and no longer free. The youth on maturity, however, would in his turn become an *eromenos* engaging in sexual-mentoring relations with adolescents as a way of maintaining the tight homosocial bonds of the democracy.

When he grew up, the youth had to move beyond this phase of homoerotic relations with an older man to become a citizen himself. He was expected to marry and thus become what we can term the head of household. Unlike the contemporaneous Spartan warrior who as an adult lived his mature life with men in martial barracks or on military campaign, the Athenian entered the fullness of citizenship by living in his domestic establishment structured not as a nuclear family but as a single economic unit usually comprising his wife, concubines, children, dependent relatives, and slaves. Maintaining this complex household was considered one of the unquestioned duties of manhood. His responsibilities included providing a dowry for daughters and raising sons in the Athenian virtues of mind and body so they could, in their turn, take on the duties of democratic citizenship. Head of household, then, was yet another role that, performed with moderation and trustworthiness, contributed to the complex fullness of Athenian manliness.

Although Athenian marriages could exhibit affectionate relations between husband and wife, they were not grounded in erotic attraction but rather in dynastic and economic considerations. In the dominant middle-class manliness of our own American society, the primary identity of man is as husband, breadwinner, and father; any divergence from monogamy would disrupt that manly role. For the Athenians, there was no opprobrium attached to sexual relations outside of marriage. Indeed, the married man had an erotic life combining both the homoerotic and the heterosexual. As a married man, man-boy relations could continue but with the roles reversed. But of course, the married man was no longer the youthful *erastes* employing his sexual power over the adult male, but the *eromenos* with the power of the adult citizen and with the duty of mentoring the young. A man was expected also to have sexual relations with professional female prostitutes, even to have a consistent relation with one of them. Paying money for sex with a prostitute was not a cause of shame since women of this class were considered inferior. Sex with the wives or daughters of other citizens, on the other hand, brought shame.

This variety of sexual relations was tolerated, even considered the sign of manliness, as long as acting out sexual desire did not interfere with the legal or economic interests of the mini-state of the household in such matters as inheritance or education of the male offspring. The criterion for manliness, then, was not marital fidelity, not the choice of male or female as partner, but whether the sexual activity was carried out with moderation and without the subordination of another citizen. The manly man could have sex in marriage with his wife, outside of marriage with female prostitutes, and with youths born as citizens as long as sexual desire did not overcome his reason, thereby making him unfit for his social obligations in the democracy.

Homosociality and Manly Moderation

As much as marriage was a duty of a citizen, Athenian society was still an intensely homosocial world. For Athenian men, their primary affective bonds were with other men. These male-male bonds were developed in youth by the eroticized man-boy relation and continued in adult life as men participated now as the *eromenos* in the mentoring of adolescents. The city-state was bound through what the Greeks called *philia,* a term for connections among men that we sadly lack and that registers deep affection or love that can, but not necessarily does, include sensual attraction. The loyalty of men in battle exemplifies *philia* as does the comradeship of Athenian democracy. Male identity resides within the male relations informed by *philia*. Indeed, the citizens felt their democracy was strengthened and sustained by this affective feeling, informed by homoeroticism.

In Plato's *Symposium* a participant states, in contrast to some contemporary American arguments against allowing gays in the military, that homoerotic bonds strengthen martial manliness:

> If there was any mechanism for producing a city or army consisting of lovers and boyfriends, there could be no better form of social organization than this: they would hold back from anything disgraceful and compete for honor in each other's eyes. If even small numbers of such men fought side by side, they could defeat virtually the whole human race. The last person a lover could bear to be seen by, when leaving his place in the battle-line or abandoning his weapons, is his boyfriend.[16]

Even beyond the battlefield, the survival of democratic rule when threatened by tyrants was seen as depending upon the homoerotic bonds of community among men. In *The Symposium,* Pausanias quite interestingly argues that intense personal love between men prevents the dissolution of democracy into despotism, the rule of one rather than the rule of the *demos*. By focusing personal emotion on other men rather than on the despot, an erotic life with many men prevents worship and obedience to a single ruler. Pausanias references the empire of Persia, the Athenians' primary enemy and to them the epitome of tyranny. In the kingdom of Persia, love affairs are forbidden so that all affect can be centered on the king. One thinks here of the antisex league in George Orwell's *1984*; romantic love is prohibited in that totalitarian state so that all can, instead, love Big Brother.[17]

> In the Persian Empire the rule is that love-affairs are wrong. In Persia, it is because of their tyrannical government that they condemn them, as well as intellectual and athletic activities. No doubt, it doesn't suit their government that their subjects should have big ideas or develop strong friendships and personal bonds, which are promoted by all these activities, especially by love. . . . So where there is a general rule that it is wrong to gratify lovers, this can be attributed to the defects of those who make this rule: the government's lust for rule and the subjects' cowardice.[18]

Yet, even such bonding among men was expected to obey the unwritten code of manly moderation. In *The Symposium* we have a fictionalized account from Plato of a symposium or all-male drinking party, a popular form of socializing for Athenian citizens. Here, elite men lie about on couches at an ancient form of the dinner party, drinking wine, and philosophizing. These parties exhibiting oratorical skills and polymorphous sexual pleasure were the exclusive preserve of men. Women, except for flute-girls, high-end prostitutes who provided both music and sexual favors, were excluded.

Plato's famous account of this all-male social event gives us a sense of the unwritten codes governing how a man behaves with other men. This is not the drunken frat party on a vast scale of drinking and feasting that bound together Viking warriors. The Athenians, reclining on their couches, choose a philosophical subject, the meaning of Eros manifested in the beauty of young men. Each man speaks on the subject with presentations ranging from the rambling to the poetic. It is the fictionalized Socrates who provides the manly ideal of the philosophical mind as moving as if on a staircase from the carnal pleasures of wooing boys to general truths about the perception of beauty in eternal transcendent forms.[19]

What is noteworthy in *The Symposium* is the implied ideal of manliness in the citizen. This fictional party is suffused with *philia* as friendship among men. This social gathering is a microcosm of the democratic state as citizens in their private lives exhibit the qualities of the citizen. They employ rhetorical eloquence, rather than force, to persuade their equals in an open forum. And Socrates exhibits the highest ideal, along with his martial skills, through his manifestation of *paideia* in posing questions that bring others to a higher truth.

In the rhetorical structure of *The Symposium,* Socrates exemplifies manly moderation of the passions and personal control of desire. His self-control and philosophical mind is set against the unmanly lack of self-discipline in Socrates's one-time disciple, Alcibiades. The tempered intellectual discussion, albeit warmed by wine, is interrupted by the intrusion of an intemperate Alcibiades who is, quite simply, drunk. The handsome young man is crowned with ivy as the manifestation of Dionysus the god of wine, of ecstatic self-transcendence, orgiastic sexual rites, and of madness:

> They heard the voice of Alcibiades in the courtyard; he was very drunk and was shouting loudly. . . . He was brought in, supported by the flute-girl and some of the other people in his group. He stood by the door, wearing a thick garland of ivy and violets, with masses of ribbons trailing over his head, and said:

"Good evening, gentlemen. Will you let someone who's drunk—very drunk—join your symposium?"[20]

For the Athenians, the ability to imbibe moderately was an indicator of manliness. Men who did not drink were unmanly; men who drank too much were also unmanly. Citizens engaging in the social rite of drinking wine at the banquet must be able to hold their liquor so they can maintain and preserve their intellectual powers and their ability to speak eloquently. Socrates personifies this moderation; Alcibiades says of him, "However much you tell him to drink, he drinks without getting drunk."[21] The entrance of the drunken Alcibiades implicitly comments on how manliness can easily be lost if one gives in to one's desires for pleasure.

Along with drinking, sex with boys, with men, and with women was valued as a natural source of pleasure but only if enjoyed in manly moderation. Alcibiades represents the unmanly immoderate expression of sexual desire as he rambles drunkenly about his homoerotic love for Socrates. Again, it is not same-sex desire that is unmanly but its potential for bringing on the disintegration of the self. The self-control of Eros for Socrates as narrated by Alcibiades shows manliness as the victory over desire:

> I threw my arms around the really god-like and amazing man [Socrates], and lay there with him all night long.... After I'd done all this, he completely triumphed over my good looks—and despised, scorned and insulted them—although I placed a very high value on these looks.... I swear to you by the gods, and by the goddesses, that when I got up the next morning I had no more *slept with* Socrates, than if I'd been sleeping with my father or elder brother.
>
> ... Although I felt I'd been humiliated, I admired his character, his self-control and courage.[22]

As an ethical fable of manliness, then, *The Symposium* shows as embodied in Socrates in full or partial contrast to the other participants, the ideals of Athenian democratic manliness—persuasive eloquence, *paideia* as the philosophical mind, sexual temperance, control of desire—all as realized within both public and private life lived within an intensely bonded society of men. In contrast, the loss of restraint is dangerous not only to the male self but also to the city-state in violating the unwritten codes of honor, in undermining the commonality of values, and in putting self-interest above the interest of the *polis*. In real life, Alcibiades served for the Athenians as the exemplar of unmanliness in his self-interest and lack of judgment, as seen in his failed generalship and his ultimate defection to Sparta.

Pericles, Exemplary Democratic Man

The fullness of Athenian manhood is exemplified in the life of Pericles: champion of democratic government, elected leader of the city-state, commander in war, statesman in the ongoing conflicts with other states, builder of the Parthenon, and patron of the drama. The fifth century BCE, the "golden age" of Athens, is often called "the Age of Pericles."

Pericles was born into the Athenian citizen elite. His father was an Athenian general; his mother came from one of the wealthiest and most politically connected of Athenian families. With this heritage, Pericles devoted his life to the highest form of Athenian manhood—serving the democratic city-state in domestic politics, in war, and in supporting the arts. Such a career of responsible duty demanded the fullest development of the mind and body to fit the man to the multiple roles of the citizen. So as a youth, Pericles, like other elite citizens, practiced music to develop an inner harmony, joined in physical exercise as training for war, and took to the reading and singing of Homeric literature for its moral values and as training for public oratory. Unlike many of his comrades, however, the young Pericles chose to spend time in the company of prominent philosophers, absorbing from these older men the valued calmness of the philosophic mind.

As an entry into public life of the democracy, the young Pericles participated in the People's Court where he used the oratorical power honed in his education to address the juries, ordinary citizens chosen by lot. Many of his cases involved the prosecution of politicians for corruption of the democratic state. Soon, on the strength of his oratorical skills, his integrity, and his intelligence, Pericles became a leader in the politics of Athens.

And since Athens was engaged in almost continuous warfare, most often with other city-states, service to the state involved military leadership. Here, Pericles, like other citizens, took on the role of warrior. Trained like all Athenian youths through compulsory military service in youth and indoctrinated in the warrior values manifested in Homeric epic, Pericles joined military expeditions where, according to the classical writer Plutarch, he showed himself "brave and fond of danger."[23] Later in his life, as a commander Pericles led most of these expeditions on land and sea himself and continued to join other citizens on the battleground. In keeping with the Athenian ideal of manliness and in contrast to the politicians and generals of our own day, as a leader Pericles donned his armor for combat.

As the leader of men in war, Pericles exhibited the self-restraint of the Athenian in his concern for their safety. Not for him the heady uncontrollable battle rage and search for glorious death in battle of the Norse warrior. Plutarch says of him, "In his generalship he was especially famous for his caution. He never willingly undertook a battle that involved great risk or uncertainty, nor did he envy or emulate those who took great risks, won brilliant successes, or were admired as great generals. He always said to his fellow-citizens that as far as it was in his power they would live forever and be immortals."[24] Here we should remember that Athenian military leaders were directly elected by and dismissed by votes of the *demos.* His continued reelection, even after military defeats, testifies to his charismatic leadership. The well-being of the city-state depended not only on military victories but on complex and shifting political alliances with other states. Pericles combined the courage of the warrior with the supple mind of the diplomat, finding great success in expanding the Athenian Empire and concluding a peace with Persia.

In his victories and his defeats on the battlefield and in diplomatic councils, Pericles was consistently devoted to preserving and strengthening the participatory democracy that he saw as the defining virtue of his city. At no time in his long career of political leadership, in times both of his embrace by the *demos* and his rejection by it, did he move to any actions that would weaken such democratic rule or bring back government by the tyrant. As Donald Kagan, the biographer of Pericles, states, "Pericles was not the founder or inventor of democracy, but he came to its leadership only a half-century after its invention, when it was still fragile. Here he certainly played the chief role in transforming it from a limited democracy where the common people still deferred to their aristocratic betters to a fully confident popular government in which the mass of the people were fully sovereign."[25] He was one of the leaders of a group advocating expanding participation by all the people rather than concentrating power in a wealthy aristocracy. Under his leadership, Athens extended involvement of citizens by providing that decisions be made in the Assembly and the courts by majority vote and that most holders of public office be chosen by lot. He expanded the work of the *demos* by authorizing small payments for the administrative Council and for the large citizen juries in the People's Courts. As in the current American system, payment for legislators and for jury service enables citizens to engage in administration and lawgiving without losing income and avoids limiting the administration of power to the wealthy. Furthermore, Pericles enabled payment for the Athenian citizen-soldiers.

Strengthener of democratic principles, elected leader of the democracy, statesman, soldier, and general, Pericles's manly service extended also to the

St. Charles Community College Library
WITHDRAWN

full realization of *paideia* in the arts. For Pericles, as for all elite citizens, a full manliness integrated not only the courage of the warrior and wiliness of the statesman but also the comprehension of beauty, not only in the male body but also in architecture, sculpture, and drama. He sponsored a tragedy by Aeschylus and was a friend of Sophocles, the author of *Oedipus Rex.* As leader, even in times of war he worked to make the city of Athens the most beautiful, the most intellectually vital, and architecturally magnificent of all cities. Indeed, he saw the city and its architecture as a material testament to the values of the democratic state. Pericles directed Athens in a huge building program on the Acropolis, the rocky hill in the center of the city, on which arose what are among the most wonderful buildings of the West. Without his encouragement, there would be no Parthenon nor the Parthenon frieze (now in the British Museum).[26] In the interior of the Parthenon stood a towering gold statue of Athena, famed in the classical world and now destroyed, commissioned from the sculptor Pheidias by his good friend Pericles. Athena was the goddess not only of the traditional values of agricultural fertility and of victory in war, but also of the qualities of Periclean Athens—wisdom, reason, and beauty. It is striking, too, that in contrast to earlier times, the frieze around the interior of the Parthenon shows not gods but the people of Athens, women as well as men in the Panathenaic procession bringing offerings to the goddess. The temple, built by Pericles, manifests the Athenian ideal that humanity has taken the place of gods.

In his justly famous "Funeral Oration," Pericles proclaimed that the richness of the Athenian manhood that he embodied—of service to the state and to beauty, of contemplation, and of action—was made possible by the principles of democracy that opened self-development to all free-born men:

> Its administration favours the many instead of the few; this is why it is called a democracy. If we look to the laws, they afford equal justice to all in their private differences; if not social standing, advancement in public life falls to reputation for capacity, class considerations not being allowed to interfere with merit; nor again does poverty bar the way, if a man is able to serve the state, he is not hindered by the obscurity of his condition. The freedom which we enjoy in our government extends also to our ordinary life.[27]

The Legacy of Athenian Manliness

Athenian manliness as exemplified in the life of Pericles lived on as an ideal in the democracies that rose in the West over two thousand years. Although perhaps none of our presidents may have achieved the fullness of Periclean manhood, the founding fathers, especially George Washington and Thomas Jefferson, fashioned their lives on the Athenian model of manliness as citizen-soldier, builder of democratic values, public servant, statesman, and benefactor of the arts.

Like Pericles, Washington gave up his life as a wealthy planter to take on his responsibilities in shaping the new republic. He commanded the Revolutionary army in the field, winning American independence against great odds. When he became the first president of the new nation, again like Pericles, he rejected the opportunity to become what the Greeks called a tyrant and instead initiated republican values. Quite strikingly, when asked what he as president was to be called, he replied "Mr. President," a sign that he was still a citizen, serving only for a time as leader. And after his two terms in office, again with the sense of Athenian participatory democracy that all citizens could serve, he retired to his country estate to resume the role of farmer.

Perhaps it is Jefferson, the third president of the United States, who comes closest to the Periclean ideal of polymath and politician fusing self-development with service to the country. He sought in his own self the ideal of *paideia* while governing his state and his nation. He served as governor of Virginia, as head of its armies in the Revolutionary War, as statesman negotiating the crucial relation of the new nation with France, and as president. His beloved home on a hill, Monticello, contains a library vast for its time. Jefferson read widely in ancient philosophy and contemporary sciences that he applied to his own farming. He sent out the Lewis and Clark expedition to the new American West partly as an imperial mission and also as a scientific and geological expedition with the hope of finding alive the dinosaurs whose fossils he collected at Monticello.

The deeply moving self-written words on his gravestone show his devotion to the Athenian ideal of democracy as grounded in independence of the society from tyrannical control; in the necessary individual freedom, particularly here the freedom to worship; and in the need to enlarge *paideia* in America through the Athenian practice of education in the liberal arts. His words encapsulate his Athenian sense of his accomplishments as a democratic man:

HERE WAS BURIED/ THOMAS JEFFERSON/ AUTHOR OF THE/

DECLARATION OF AMERICAN INDEPENDENCE/ OF THE STATUTE OF VIRGINIA FOR

RELIGIOUS FREEDOM/AND FATHER OF THE/

UNIVERSITY OF VIRGINIA/ BORN APRIL 2, 1743 O.S./ DIED JULY 4. 1826

Indeed, the foundational speech of American history, Lincoln's Gettysburg Address, in its praise of democratic values and of the deeds of the soldier dead in maintaining these values quite consciously draws upon the "Funeral Oration" of Pericles and reasserts for a reunited America the values of Athenian manhood.[28] As Pericles stated of the Athenians lost in war, so Lincoln over two thousand years later declared that honor and glory and renown now must go to the soldiers who died at Gettysburg as defenders of democracy:

> Four score and seven years ago our fathers brought forth on this continent a new nation, conceived in liberty, and dedicated to the proposition that all men are created equal.
>
> It is for us the living, rather, to be dedicated here to the unfinished work which they who fought here have thus far so nobly advanced. It is rather for us to be here dedicated to the great task remaining before us—that from these honored dead we take increased devotion to that cause for which they gave the last full measure of devotion—that we here highly resolve that these dead shall not have died in vain—that this nation, under God, shall have a new birth of freedom—and that government of the people, by the people, for the people, shall not perish from the earth.

Chapter 3

The Craftsman

As Achilles prepares for battle against the Trojans, his mother, the goddess Thetis, eager to provide invincible armor for her son, seeks out Hephaestus, patron god of workers in metal. Thetis pleads:

> Give my son—he won't live long—
> A shield and helmet and tooled greaves with ankle-straps
> and armor for his chest. (18: 534–36)

Hephaestus agrees and, in one of the most celebrated sections of the *Iliad,* with heroic effort he shapes the fabled shield of Achilles, a wonder of beauty and protection:

> And first Hephaestus makes a great and massive shield,
> blazoning well-wrought emblems all across its surface,
> raising a rim around it, glittering, triple-ply
> with a silver shield-strap run from edge to edge
> and five layers of metal to build the shield itself,
> and across its vast expanse with all his craft and cunning
> the god creates a world of gorgeous immortal work. (18: 558–64)

It is this masterpiece of metalworking with its portrayal of the constellations, the earth, and of contrasting cities on which the life of this paragon of warriors depends. In their death struggle, the spear of Hector cannot penetrate the shield of Achilles. Hector dies; Achilles survives.

And yet the figure of the god Hephaestus, the master worker in metal, says much of the valuation of the craftsman in classical society and, by extension, in our own world. As necessary as his skill may be to a warrior society, Hephaestus, the protector of the warrior, is deficient in the high attributes of warrior manliness. If Achilles is the epitome of warrior physicality, Hephaestus is physically deformed. A worker at the forge, he is immensely strong in his upper body with powerful arms, but his legs are weak, atrophied because of his labor:

> his immense hulk
> hobbling along but his shrunken legs moved nimbly . . .
> then he sponged off his brow and both burly arms,
> his massive neck and shaggy chest, pulled on a shirt
> and grasping a heavy staff, Hephaestus left his forge
> and hobbled on. (18: 480–81, 485–88)

In a society that worshipped male bodily beauty, lameness signified a deficiency of manliness.

Deformed in body, Hephaestus is also deficient in sexual prowess. Hephaestus was married to Aphrodite, the goddess of love. Yet because of his grotesque body, he was cuckolded. Aphrodite slept with Ares, the god of war and of warriors. For revenge, Hephaestus, the worker in metal, prepared a net of chain mail in which he entangled them in the act of sex. But when the craftsman god brought the naked bodies of the god of war and the goddess of love to the assembled gods, they did not punish the lovers but merely laughed, then freed Ares and Aphrodite. Hephaestus as deformed craftsman was an unmanly man who deserved his cuckoldry.

The granting of godhood to the worker in metals suggests the value that the classical world placed on the craftsman. But Hephaestus is a diminished man. His identity as an essential worker is tied to unmanly deficiencies bound up with the very nature of his work. His status as god affirms the skill and the necessity of the craftsman while simultaneously assigning this masculine identity a secondary place within the society. As we shall see, this mix of both valuing and denigrating the craftsman runs from the age of Homer through the Athenian democracy to our own privileging of what we term art over craft.

Craftsman as Masculine Identity

How then can we define the craftsman as a form of masculine identity continuing through history from the Homeric world, to classical Athens and through the European Renaissance, and into the machine age?

As a generality, we can say that a craftsman is a man whose primary self-definition as well as his definition by society depends upon his skillful practice of making something well. Hephaestus as craftsman-god fulfilled a clear social function crucial to a warrior society that depended upon hand-forged metals for the armor of warriors. The craftsman, whether god or mortal, is defined by his mastery of *technē,* a useful Greek term for craft denoting the application of knowledge to the production of material forms. Before the rise of the machine in the late eighteenth and early nineteenth centuries, craft or *technē* was intimately bound to the skill of the hand. In our postindustrial era where machines have, for the most part, taken over the act of making, the word *craft* still implies the skilled use of the hand.

Yet it can be argued that in our postindustrial computerized age, the term *craft* should be extended beyond handwork to expert work in general. Richard Sennett, for example, argues in *The Craftsman* that "craftsmanship cuts a far wider swath than skilled manual labor: it serves the computer programmer, the doctor, and the artist; parenting improves when it is practiced as a skilled craft."[1] This redefinition of craft as applied expertise is provocative, especially in expanding the definition of a masculine identity as craftsman into our own time when material objects can be created by machine. *Technē* might now apply to the nonmaterial as in work with computers. And yet since the subject of this volume is on the history of the self-being of men as defined internally and by social modes, I will focus on those occupations traditionally defined as craft: those enterprises of men working with the skilled hand and body to shape material forms.

Some elements in the formation and the activity of man as craftsman do remain consistent through history. In all times, the craftsman achieves his expertise not through sudden inspiration, but through a long period of training, usually in the form of an apprenticeship. Through this apprenticeship, he absorbs the rules and techniques of his craft. Paradoxically, only by mastering the tradition can he inform his making with traces of his own personality. Rather than privileging romantic individualism, craft emphasizes bringing the personal touch to objects produced within traditional means. In contrast to our own ideal inherited from nineteenth-century romanticism of creation as depending on individual effort, the craftsman, whether Athenian potter or medieval goldsmith, collaborates with others. The site of craft is not the isolated studio but the workshop that includes other workers with greater or lesser skills and responsibilities.

A mode of personal and social identity for men, the role of craftsman is defined by certain qualities that are, again, consistent through history. As uncompromising dedication to honor marks the warrior, so uncompromising dedication to honest skilled work defines the craftsman. What might be called the code of the craftsman calls for integrity in making: whether in dying wool, in building the house frame, or in riveting the girders of high steel. Expertise applied well and honestly marks the essential identity of man as craftsman and cannot be compromised without destroying the self. Even in our capitalist society, for the modern craftsman such as the master plumber or electrician, the imperative for the self is not to make money, though plumbers and electricians do well but to do well by doing good, not shoddy, work. For the craftsman, making is the basis of his being, the primary activity of his life, not a hobby, as craft has become in our own world where the woodworking shop in the basement serves as a refuge from the corporate office.

The craftsman must prove his manhood by exhibiting the product of his skilled labor for his peers and by following a code of honor in his work—using only the most appropriate materials and providing the best and most focused expertise. In doing so, he is participating in an identity shared with other men. For craftsmen live within social structures that enforce and recognize craftsmanship and that bring the individual into a manly fellowship. The associations of Athens, the medieval guilds, and the professional organizations of electricians and of physicians regulate training and practice as well as recognize an achieved expertise, thereby providing a social grounding for individual identity. As in all times, masculine identity involves not only a set of personal skills but a valuing of such skills in the social world beyond the self.

It is worth noting that if craftsman describes a masculine identity, there is no parallel term for women. Neither in the past nor in the present do we speak of craftswomen. The absence of this term is particularly striking since from Homeric times to the beginnings of the machine age, women practiced the skills that define the "crafts-man," specifically in the expert handwork of making textiles and producing clothing. From ancient Greece to preindustrial America, women spun raw wool on the hand-operated spinning wheel in the home, hence the term spinster, and on the domestic handloom transformed this yarn into fabric and then into clothing. Such skilled work defined female identity, as in the story of Penelope weaving and then destroying fabric woven on her loom as she awaited the return of Odysseus from Troy. But since such highly skilled activity was relegated to the domestic, rather than operating in the public sphere, in a highly patriarchal society women's work as weaver was granted little value. To equate the skilled manual work of the woman with the craft work of a man would be to dissolve the sex distinction that grounded patriarchal society. Indeed, the patriarchal function of valorizing craft performed by men persists as in the intense resistance to allowing women into contemporary craft guilds such as the carpenters or electricians unions. For many, craft still remains a defining identity limited to men.

Defining the craftsman must engage the complex historical issue of the distinction between craft and art, between the craftsman and the artist. We now tend to see craft as the making of a functional or useful object in distinction to art as the making of an object valuable for its own sake and without utility. To the contemporary mind, there is a difference between crafting a vessel for drinking wine or armor for protection, in contrast to painting a portrait called the *Mona Lisa* or rendering a woman pouring milk in a Dutch interior. In the classical world and through the Renaissance, this distinction between craft and art simply did not exist: "The most obvious indication of this conceptual difference being given by the language. In Greek, *technē* and, in Latin, *ars* were used indiscriminately of painting and cobbling alike."[2]

Furthermore, the distinction between craft and art is inherently problematic since functional objects have a supplement that is wholly nonfunctional. The many-layered impenetrable shield of Achilles with its nonfunctional engravings of landscapes and cities is a case in point. Ancient Greek vases, as we shall see, provide a perfect conundrum for the craft vs. art distinction. The vessels function for mixing wine with water and for drinking at such events as the symposium described by Plato. But they are decorated with figures of red or black with scenes of gods and men that are among the most compelling aesthetic achievements of world art. In the Renaissance, the Italian Benvenuto Cellini (1500–71) made a salt cellar of gold, enamel, and ivory for Francis I of France. The salt container is topped with the figures of a naked sea god and a woman sitting opposite each other with legs entwined, symbolically representing the planet Earth. This container to hold salt at royal banquets expands so far beyond the function of holding salt that we tend to call it a "work of art."[3] During the Renaissance, in Italy men did not limit their self-definition to the binary of craftsman or artist but rather moved between the self-contained aesthetic and the useful, often combining both, as in the example of Cellini. Leonardo da Vinci, as it is well known, did not do only frescoes and easel paintings but also designed fortifications and sketched plans for water pumps, flying machines, and parachutes.

Indeed the Renaissance artist was closer to a master craftsman than to the current image of the artist. Painting was seen as a matter of skill rather than inspiration. In the workshop, the categories of craftsman and artist were fused. Expertise in procedures and methods had to be acquired through long training. And this expertise was achieved only through lengthy apprenticeship to a master. At the age of fourteen, Leonardo was apprenticed to the master painter Verrocchio. In Verrochio's atelier, he learned how to mix paints and prepare surfaces. As his competence increased, he was allowed to paint details in the work of his master. At the conclusion of this regimen, he became a master himself in the Guild of St. Luke, the guild for artists.

The split between craftsman and artist, between craft and art that governs our own thinking, derives from the romantic sensibility that emerged in Europe at the end of the eighteenth and beginning of the nineteenth century. In a sense, romanticism deskilled the process of making what we now call "art." This romantic mode, in theory at least, sees the creation of art as flowing from moments of inspiration in states of heightened awareness. Art becomes valued as the expression of intense inward states. Traditionally, craft depends on expertise developed through long training. In the romantic view, the creator as artist is a person of intense sensibility, rather than one who has mastered a complex set of skills. Making, then, becomes secondary to expression. Vincent van Gogh is an exemplary painter for the intensity of the expression of his self in his own personal renderings of olive trees or wheat fields. Jackson Pollock consciously eschewed craftsmanship for expression in drip paintings where he seemingly unconsciously poured commercially prepared paint onto canvas spread on the floor. Art as depending on the acquisition of traditional technique has been replaced by art as intensity and originality.

Man as craftsman, a self-identity gained through learning traditions and techniques, becomes separated from man as artist whose identity derives from his sensitivity and originality expressed without the need for training in skills. This divergence between craftsman and artist is embedded in our distinction between high art and low art, between the modern artist and the modern craftsman, and in the diminished value of skilled work done by the hand.

The Craftsman in the Classical World

Forms of manliness emerge because they are functional. For a society whose primary occupations were war and agriculture, each depending on strong muscles and iron implements—swords and shields, plows and scythes—

the worker in iron was crucial. The Greeks elevated the ironworker into a god, albeit a lame one. A hymn of the ancient Greeks attributed to Homer praises this god of craftsmen and asserts the dependence of civilization on craft: "Sing, clear-voiced Muses, of Hephaestus famed for inventions. With bright-eyed Athene he taught men glorious gifts throughout the world,— men who before used to dwell in caves in the mountains like wild beasts. But now that they have learned crafts through Hephaestus the famed worker, easily they live a peaceful life in their own houses the whole year round."[4] And yet the tale of the cuckolding of Hephaestus by Ares indicates that in the value system of the ancient world, the craftsman ranked lower in the hierarchy of manliness than the warrior. The strength of his arm at the forge did not translate into manly virility.

Within the city-state of Athens in the sixth, fifth, and fourth centuries BCE, workers in iron were included in a distinct social group termed *banausoi* defined as those who practiced *technē* or the practical work of making. Such social categorization through language shows that for the Athenians, those who practiced *technē* exhibited a clearly defined form of male identity. In a fashion that might appear inconsistent to the contemporary mind, the *banausoi* included those we would now categorize as craftsmen, skilled practitioners in making functional objects—nail-makers, tanners, dyers of cloth—as well as those we would term artisans, makers of functional yet decorative articles—goldsmiths, jewelers, potters, vase-painters, and glass-blowers. Also defined as *banausoi* were those we would now consider artists—sculptors and vase-painters. The category included as well those we call architects since building was then seen as a hands-on skill. Within Athenian discourse, what these men had in common was translating abstract thought into material form, and as such differed from and were considered inferior to the philosophers such as Plato, who dealt wholly with the realm of abstractions and ideas.[5]

In the classical world, the *banausoi* achieved a social identity by organizing into groups with membership defined by a trade. In Athens, members of the *banausoi* formed cult organizations limited to specific crafts such as carpentry, leatherworking, and dyeing whose purpose was less economic gain for the group than mutual participation in religious rites. In the Roman world, craftsmen could join a group called a *collegium* open to men of a specific occupation where the organizing principle was mutual social obligation such as paying for funerals.[6]

Craftsmen also asserted their group identity in the public sphere. In civic processions in the Roman city of Pompeii, craftsmen such as blacksmiths and carpenters were given a place of honor along with images of gods. A preserved wall painting shows woodworkers in such a public spectacle carrying on their shoulders a portable platform showing their patron goddess, Minerva, as well as representations of carpenters at work: one planing a piece of wood and two together sawing a wooden plank.[7] Such Greek and Roman associations are continuous with later all-male organizations such as the medieval guilds and nineteenth-century craft unions that provided social identity as well as practical benefits to skilled workers.

As with all forms of masculine identity, the social definition fuses with and supports the personal sense of self. Although the classical skilled worker was often not literate, and if literate not given to introspection, there is some evidence of internalized self-worth grounded in the craftsman's pride in his skill. The classical craftsman often signed his work. As early as the seventh century BCE, the sculptor Euthykartides signed his name to a monument as did the later Greek vase-painter Chares of Corinth. An individual mason cut his name into a building block of the Parthenon.[8] This marking of one's name on his made object asserts the self-worth of a man as manifested in his mastery of *technē*, his skill as maker. As Alison Burford, the chronicler of the classical craftsman eloquently states, "The same intention always underlay the act of signing—the craftsman was saying in effect, 'Here is my answer to the technical and stylistic problems presented by this piece of work.'"[9]

And yet, even though their skill was granted recognition in the public sphere, to classical society craftsmen appeared to inhabit an inferior form of manliness. Of course, this denigration of the worker came not from the craftsmen themselves who, as we have seen, took pride in their craft, but from wealthy people who did not have to labor with their hands for a living. The elite of Athens and Rome valued the beauty of the male body and looked to an ideal physique manifested in their statuary such as the Discobolus as the sign of manliness.[10] Perhaps to justify the class system of the society, the craftsman was assigned a lower form of manliness by pointing to his seemingly malformed body shaped into deformity by the necessities of his work. The lame legs and huge upper body of Hephaestus provide a case in point. To the Greek elite, the excessive musculature developed in certain activities, such as that of quarrymen, seemed a divergence from the ideals of male bodily beauty. A typical comment is that of the Athenian Xenophon: "banausic activities . . . spoil the bodies of the workmen and the overseers, because the nature of the work compels them to sit indoors. . . . Softening of the body leads to softening of the mind."[11]

As Xenophon implies, for the Athenian elite the sound body was valued for strengthening the mind. For the Athenians, as we have seen, the highest goal of life was the development of a philosophic mind. For Plato, there was a ladder of ascent from occupation with the material world to a vision of the eternal immaterial "Forms" that ground our physical senses. The ideal of *paideia* sees education as leading to the abstract realms of ideas rather than to the skill of the hand. This denigration of working in materials and in things continues with what many feel is a harmful effect into our own discourse of education where, for example, vocational training is deemed inferior to liberal education and set aside for those of inferior class status.[12]

For the craftsmen of the classical world, as for craftsmen in general, their expertise was acquired through long and arduous training through apprenticeship. In contrast to our own tradition of the new, craftsmanship was defined by existing tradition rather than innovation. In Greece and Rome such acquisition of skill occurred within the family; secrets of the craft, as in the formulas for dyeing or for tanning leather, were passed down from father to son, from generation to generation without change. Even in our own world, with all its ostensible social mobility, certain skilled work is continued within families. In coal mining in England and America, a skilled if highly dangerous occupation, sons follow their fathers into the mines. For firemen or construction workers at a skilled level such as bolters in high steel, there is continuity as sons follow fathers into the craft.

This training and the practice of the craftsman in the classical world took place within a busy gathering of workers, rather than a solitary studio. Another wall painting from Pompeii shows a workshop of woolworkers. Two men comb the wool of a sheepskin. Nearby four men collaborate in making a waterproof felt by using a glue to bind wool with animal hair. Another man, presumably the master of this workshop, holds up a finished felt and provides his name, "Verecundus," under his product for sale.[13]

Like the Roman woolen waterproof, the celebrated vases of the Greek and Roman world also emerged from a workshop. Ancient representations of the potter's craft show a complex process involving activities dangerous and tedious, unskilled and highly skilled. There is the digging and transporting of the clay and the shaping of the wet clay on the wheel. Only then does the vase-painter, the closest approximation to our idea of the artist, apply the figures to the surface. Guided by the expertise of the master potter, workers bring the kiln to the correct intensity of heat to fire the clay and glaze followed by the reduction in heat to bring out the glaze, all to be done with care and accuracy lest the pot or vase disintegrate.[14] Although a master craftsman might be occupied with one specialty, for example vase-painting, he had to be knowledgeable about all these phases of production, even if they were carried out by less-skilled workers.

As we have noted, the making of pottery in the classical world presents a complex case of the merging of what we now term craft and art. Ordinary bowls and storage vessels such as the amphora, large thin-necked vessels used to store and transport such goods as olives and wine, were strictly utilitarian in purpose and served the general population. These clay vessels were unglazed and undecorated. If we apply modern categories, these vessels can be considered within the category of craft as manufactured by skilled handwork in a workshop.

But for the elites, vessels—especially for drinking and mixing wine— were painted and glazed, often with scenes of great beauty depicting mythological events, Homeric episodes or figures from the Olympic Games. Such vases demanded not only the craft of the workshop, but also what we must term the aesthetic prowess of a single vase-painter. Such individuals often signed their work and, if not, can be identified by stylistic evidence. Although produced by a group of craftsmen in a workshop and serving useful functions, these vases fit our own definition of art since they include the work of a single man of genius. As art, Greek vases now have pride of place in our museums. But we must remember that for the Greeks, though not for us, the distinction between craft and art did not exist. For the ancient world the categories of craftsman and artist were combined into one person or, more accurately, into a group of persons of varied degrees of skill.

As the example of classical workshops demonstrates, for the Greeks and Romans there was a certain degree of what we would call specialization in craftwork. Some men worked in stone, others in wood, and others in gold or leather or metal. And as the example of the vase-painter indicates, there was some degree of specialization within the potter's workshop. Yet the classical craftsman, unhampered by the rigid laws of the medieval guilds or the sharp division of labor in mechanized factories, engaged in a broad range of activity. A craftsman in wood could work on a brick wall or even as a laborer in erecting scaffolding. This jack-of-all-trades quality among classical craftsmen arose since many works were done by teams gathered for a specific project. For example, the building of the great monuments of classical Athens, such as the Erechtheion, a temple on the Acropolis next to the Parthenon, was done by a team including highly specialized workers such as masons, sculptors, wood-carvers, painters (Greek buildings were not white but decorated in bright colors), gilders, and laborers—each paid according to the going valuation of his specialty. Records show that each of these craftsmen pitched in for other work: a sculptor working in wood and a stone mason as a laborer in order to get the job done.[15]

In such a vast architectural project, coordination of craftwork was necessary and thus arose the need for a single person who had an overall view of the larger work to which each craftsman contributed. As the Greek and Roman temples and theaters and stadiums grew in scale, there emerged the role of a supervisor who moved away from performing handwork to become what we now term an architect or engineer. The architect-engineer began his career through training in a craft tradition rather than through theoretical learning for there were no schools for such professional training. Still, the separation of craftsman and administrator, of maker and designer, led to the bifurcation of brainwork and handwork that persists today, often to the devaluing of the craftsman.

The Craftsman in Preindustrial Europe: The Guild System

In medieval and Renaissance Europe as in classical times, the craftsman, the skilled maker, was essential to the functioning of society. The conditions of warfare had changed little from the Trojan wars. With continuing warfare between feudal lords and foreign wars such as the Crusades, metalworkers forged the armor of the knights, as well as their lances and swords. Fletchers shaped the feathered arrows for soldiers' longbows.

The manufacturing and services that enabled daily life on the farm and in the growing cities were still done by hand. These crafts were continuous with those of daily life in Athens and Rome. There were bakers, basket makers, and blacksmiths. Shoes were made and repaired by cobblers, and clothing was made by weavers who in turn depended on needle makers. Housing great and small called for carpenters, plasterers, plumbers, and masons. Domestic life depended on chandlers (candle makers), upholders (upholsterers), and cutlery makers. Food and drink was supplied by butchers and brewers. Transportation depended upon farriers to shoe the horses and wheelwrights to make the wagons. For the wealthy there were cordwainers (workers in fine leather), goldsmiths, and jewelers. Craft still depended on the passing down of traditional methods. The cobbler or blacksmith of Athens or Rome could have easily joined a workshop in medieval London or Paris.

The major change in the social position of the craftsman from the ancient world to premodern Europe lay in the social organization of his identity. Skilled workers in Greece and Rome joined social and religious groups that drew members from a particular craft, but these provided only limited mutual economic support. Beginning in the twelfth century, the social identity of the craftsman strengthened as skilled workers organized according to their craft into powerful associations called guilds. The guilds controlled and regularized training in a specific craft, established a hierarchy of achievement within the craft, and provided economic benefit to the craftsman by maintaining a strict monopoly limiting work in a craft to members of a specific guild. Furthermore, though still occupying as in Greece and Rome a middling social status, between the landowning aristocracy and the peasants, through the increasing power of their guilds craftsmen were able to maintain autonomy from feudal control. Their power increased as cities grew and capitalism generated an increasing demand for luxury commodities. In providing a social and institutional identity for the craftsman, the guild system, it must be emphasized, also strengthened the skilled handworkers' sense of personal self-worth.

The medieval guild was strictly organized by specialty. The goldsmiths, leatherworkers, and carpenters, for example, had their own guild. If a Greek or Roman craftsman might take on a number of tasks, doing masonry or carpentry or even manual labor, such working across craft lines was forbidden by the guilds. A medieval carpenter was not permitted to do the work of a mason. Craftsmen were forbidden by law to practice their skill if they were not members of a guild. By holding a monopoly on activity in their craft within each city, the guild system contributed to the financial well-being of its members.

These powers were granted to the guild by the governing authority. Thus, society transferred jurisdiction over certain forms of skilled work and workers to a nongovernmental organization. A modern analogy would be the current guild system governing physicians and lawyers. In America, federal, state, and local governments grant the medical and legal establishment control over training, certification within the profession, and the disciplining of practitioners. Similarly, unions control entry and discipline for such craftsmen as electricians and plumbers.

In medieval Europe, the social prestige, personal self-esteem, and economic power of craftsmen was achieved through the guild's regularization of the training and the practice of each craft. This standardization created a certification system that guaranteed a specific level of competence much as the standards of medical training overseen by medical societies certify the competence of the surgeon who removes your appendix. The standards for licensing electricians in our world do much to guarantee that our fuses will not blow again after the electrician is gone. The granting of titles such as journeyman and master ratify achievement of a level of competence, as do the positions of intern, resident, and specialist for contemporary physicians. In overseeing the practice of its members, the guild system did much to prevent dishonesty or shoddy work since such work would diminish the status of all the guild members as well as the system itself. The reputation of the guild of plumbers or carpenters or joiners would be weakened and livelihood diminished by a member falling below a standard of workmanship and reliability.

As in the classical world, the skill of the medieval craftsman was attained through a long apprenticeship in the workshop. As a path to a stable career, entry into the guild system was most desirable, and limited, of course, to males. Most often, the entrance was gained through family connections; the sons of masters were entered as apprentices in the family workshop. For outsiders, entry was more difficult; parents paid or gave away their sons to a master to serve as an apprentice. Once bound as apprentice, the boy lived with the other apprentices in the dwelling of a master craftsman and his family; medieval homes served as both living space and work space. The master of the workshop thus assumed the position of parent. Harsh discipline by the master over his apprentices was common and generally accepted. Looking ahead to the industrial age, we can compare this workshop-home with its surrogate family to the separation of work and home that came about with the centralization of labor in the factory. During the apprenticeship, the future craftsman absorbed the expertise of his craft by doing lower-level work—mixing the metals, holding the tools, and preparing the clay under the supervision of the master.

After this long and demanding period of training, and if his skill was acceptable, the apprentice could move on to the next stage, journeyman. This promotion from apprentice to journeyman marked the transition from boy to adult and, as in all forms of manhood, was marked by a rite of passage to test whether the young man had the qualifications to enter a socially defined form of manhood: the masculine identity of the craftsman. To become a man within the guild system, the apprentice had to produce a piece of work that demonstrated his expertise in the traditions of the craft and certified that he could meet the standards of the guild. To climb this ladder of certification, then, the young man worked not with mental abstractions, as in our schools and universities, but on material objects shaped by the hand. Once granted the rank of journeyman, the former apprentice could now leave the workshop and "journey" as a "man" to other places. Certified at this level of expertise, he could work for other masters; sharpen his skills; and, unlike apprentices, be paid for his labor.

After journeying and with several years of experience, a journeyman could become a master craftsman in charge of his own workshop. This final rise in rank would typically require the approval of all masters of a guild as well as a donation of money and other goods to the guild. This new identity required yet another test of manhood, another rite of passage that demonstrated expertise through another qualifying work—the so-called masterpiece from which derives our contemporary use of the term. Thus a man, once he was able to enter the guild system, could move through the arduous education of the hand and mind from apprentice through journeyman to master to achieve a valued form of manhood.

The identity of the preindustrial craftsman, then, depended on a specific set of skills validated by testing before one's male equals. If the warrior manifests his own being through physical courage in battle and the Athenian in his speaking skills before the assembly of citizens, the craftsman proves his own self-worth through demonstrating the skills of his hand in making. It is this proficiency that marks the essential being of a man as craftsman from Hephaestus to the current worker in high steel in Manhattan. It is this skill and its honest practice in dyeing wool, in building the house frame, and in curing leather that defines the man and, like honor for the warrior or reputation for the Athenian, cannot be compromised without destroying the self. To turn out an inferior product for mere financial gain or hide an improperly joined dwelling frame or wagon wheel is to violate the code of this specific form of manliness.

At its best, then, a masculine identity links a personal sense of self to a larger social construction of manliness in which the man participates and from which he draws his internal feeling of worth. In the *Iliad,* the warriors are identified by their skills; Achilles is the "breaker of horses." The free-born Athenian man could say with justifiable pride, "I am a citizen of Athens," implying a set of skills and values shared with other men of the democratic city-state. The guild system provided a similar honorific, a term conveying social respect for the individual through membership in a community of men. The medieval craftsman could say, then, not merely "I am John Jones," but "I am John Jones, journeyman in leather," or "I am John Jones, master in the leather-working guild." Man is still defined by his work; and the work is validated by society. A man might now say, "I am John Jones, thoracic surgeon," or "I am John Jones, crane-operator." Thus the guild system provided a man an identity beyond his own personality that was vouched for by his self-governing organization and grounded by his demonstrated expertise in his craft. This was a stable, transportable identity that, one would imagine, bestowed a personal sense of well-being on the anxious apprentice, on the journeyman on his travels beyond his home city, and on the master craftsman training his apprentices.

The Craftsman in the Machine Age

By the late eighteenth and early nineteenth centuries, the masculine identity as craftsman—the definition of self through expertise in the skill of the hand and the validation of such expertise by a communal structure—was starkly challenged and, at best, marginalized as mechanization took over the making of material goods. First in England, then in Europe and America, the guild workshop gave way to the factory and the skill of the handworker to the self-regulating speed and consistency of the machine.

The age of invention that began in the late 1700s in England developed machines eventually powered by steam that replaced handwork.[16] The industrial revolution first transformed the weaving of textiles. Until the invention and deployment of textile machinery in England, men called handloom weavers worked at looms in their homes powering the wooden device with their feet and tossing the shuttle through the warp with their hands. The finished cloth was then collected from their homes by a trader for distribution and sale.

With the coming of mechanization, the handloom weaver as craftsman virtually disappeared, and weaving, as well as the spinning of fiber into yarn, was relocated to a central site: the factory. In these vast buildings, looms that drew their power from a stationary steam engine spun yarn on a multitude of spindles and effortlessly, tirelessly, and relentlessly drew the thread through the warp to weave finished cloth. Crucially, these machines were automatic and self-regulating. Once set in motion and fed yarn, the loom relentlessly and without error spun cloth. Neither expertise nor the skill of the hand was needed. The textile mill needed only machine watchers who did not participate in the process but remained on the alert for any breakdown. In great danger, little children darted among the moving parts of the loom to tie broken threads.

Even the skilled hand-weaving that produced complex designs in finished cloth was eliminated by the invention of a loom that operated as a proto-computer. The jacquard loom ran according to a punch-card system that anticipated the twentieth-century systems of IBM. Holes were made in cardboard sheets that when fed into a loom managed the lifting of thread as the cloth was woven. A design could then be repeated endlessly without error. Skill was relocated from the handworker to the designer of the patterns punched into cards. The weaver was now unnecessary—even for setting a pattern into cloth.

Furthermore, the factory system imposed a rigid division of labor. The preindustrial workshop operated according to a hierarchy in which workers performed different tasks. But still, as in the classical world, the workers could move from task to task as needed. In the factory, efficiency for the sake of profit ruled so that workers were set to a single repetitive task from which they could not deviate. In the factory, the worker made only one part of the manufactured object before passing the piece on to the next laborer who completed another feature through a repetitive activity, as in the assembly line of contemporary automobile production. No longer did the item bear, as in Greece and Rome, the mark of the maker as a sign of pride and skill. Rather the worker was divorced or alienated from personal engagement with the finished product. Workers on the assembly lines of factories were in the nineteenth century called "hands," a term that nicely encapsulates that within the mechanized industrial system, men were useful only for the repetitive ability of their hands, rather than of the craftsmanlike fusion of hands and mind.

Thus the craftsman became, in our own terms, redundant. Craft as we have defined it—skilled work by hand that emerges from rigorous training—was not required in the mechanized factory. The handloom weaver, the symbol in his own time of this radical shift from individual hand production, lost his vocation; instead, he became one of the first groups in history to become technologically unemployed.

Crucially, the identity of man as craftsman was itself made redundant as this great deskilling of labor took place. The preindustrial craftsman drew his identity from his expertise and his sense of worth from his ability as certified by fellow workmen in the craft. Now, in the machine age, skill was no longer needed because the worker as craftsman was transformed into the worker as unskilled employee. His worth was denoted not by mastery but by the amount of money earned, by what the nineteenth century called "cash payment." Not expertise, but the amount earned marked self-worth. The communal system of the guild gave way to control by the factory owner, now called the "master" in an ironic usurpation of the title of the head of a craft workshop. The worker was just one among many employees subject to the profit-making needs of production. Until the rise of unions, each worker competed individually with other workers in bargaining with his employer for his pay.

An eloquent account by the novelist Richard Russo of the transformation in the making of leather gloves in the town of Gloversville in central New York State, in the early twentieth century, vividly illustrates the decline of the craftsman and of craft that began in the late eighteenth century and early nineteenth with the advent of the machine. From the nineteenth century on, in this small town, gloves were made by a guild of skilled workers, many having emigrated from Italy. In this town, glove-making remained a craft endeavor in which the craftsman prided himself in his skill. Russo's grandfather worked in a now vanished world that depended on the fusion of hand and personal imagination in shaping imperfect and unique raw material:

> The primary tools of a guild-trained glove cutter's trade were his eye, his experience of animal skins, and his imagination.... He [the grandfather] explained the challenge of making something truly fine and beautiful from an imperfect animal hide. [The cured skins] retain some of nature's flaws. The true craftsman ... works around these flaws or figures out how to incorporate them into the glove's natural folds or stitching. Each skin posed a problem whose solution required imagination. The glove cutter's job wasn't just to get as many gloves as possible out of a skin but to do so while minimizing its flaws.[17]

The elimination in twentieth-century Gloversville of craft and thus of the identity of the worker as craftsman by mechanization exemplifies the process of deskilling. Once his grandfather "returned from World War II glove-making was largely mechanized by 'clicker' cutting machines that quickly stamped out pre-sized gloves, requiring the operator only to position the tanned skin under the machine's lethal blades and pull down on its mechanical arm."[18] And with the substitution of the glove-making machine for the man as glove-cutter, the craft element disappeared; the quality of the gloves deteriorated as did the psyche of the glove-maker. The former craftsman became a machine-tender and eventually lost his job. Russo describes the town of craftsman after the introduction of mechanization—the workers have departed, and only a few dispirited men linger in the barrooms. Like the English handloom weavers, their livelihood and their sense of self were gone.

In the later nineteenth century, the deskilling of man's work brought on by mechanization generated a strong oppositional movement dedicated to restoring the role of the craftsman by revaluing the worth of handmade products. Nowhere was this battle fought out more intensely than in architecture. It was the stone mason and the sculptor in stone who in constructing the great buildings of Greece and the cathedrals of medieval Europe that epitomized the merger of craft with what we could now call art. In the nineteenth century, mechanization was eliminating craft and the craftsman from the enterprise of building. This separation of architecture and craft was epitomized in the construction of a structure called the Crystal Palace, erected for a world's fair in London in 1851. The Crystal Palace was designed as a giant greenhouse of glass and iron.[19] The glass panes, iron columns, and iron beams of the Crystal Palace were prefabricated off-site by machine to exact and standardized specifications. The glass and iron components were then assembled rapidly by workers at the site. The same scheme was used to build the iron and glass train sheds of nineteenth-century railway stations, the cathedrals of the machine age. These thoroughly functional and in many ways attractive structures, the predecessors of our own steel and glass office towers wholly eliminated the craftsman from the work of building. There was no stone to sculpt. The laborers only pieced together the machine-made elements. Neither skill of the hand nor personal expression through carving was called for. Unlike the teams of craftsmen who built the Parthenon and the cathedrals, these were crews on an architectural assembly line.

Much of the nineteenth-century argument against such machine-made buildings and against machine-made commodities in general turned on the issue of uniformity vs. irregularity in the finished product. One of the essential features of the machine is its ability to reproduce exact copies endlessly. The jacquard loom could ceaselessly turn out formerly expensive hand-woven patterned cloth. Wood-carving machines could reproduce furniture formerly handcarved by members of the woodworking guilds. Imperfection, then, manifests the work of the hand and by extension, it was argued, the soul of a craftsman. In the most famous and eloquent defense of craft in the nineteenth century, "The Nature of Gothic," John Ruskin, a critic of art and of society, calls out in the voice of a biblical prophet that asking men to work as machines destroys the soul and that the valuing of imperfection will restore a manliness grounded in the fusion of hand and God-given creative energy:

> You must either make a tool of the creature, or a man of him. You cannot make both. Men were not intended to work with the accuracy of tools, to be

precise and perfect in all their actions. If you will have that precision out of them, and make their fingers measure degrees like cogwheels, and their arms strike curves like compasses, you must unhumanize them. . . . The eye of the soul must be bent upon the finger point, and the soul's force must fill all the invisible nerves that guide it.[20]

As Ruskin's admiration of the stone-carvers of medieval Gothic cathedrals exemplifies, as handcraft gave way before machine production, the remaining craftsmen in the modern landscape acquired a heroic aura informed by a sentimental nostalgia that continues into our contemporary world. The more that handicraft disappeared, the more the craftsman was evoked as an emblem of a moralized and muscular manliness lost in the machine age. Take the example of the blacksmith. The blacksmith as craftsman fashioning horseshoes and iron implements through the power of his good right arm lived in literature as an elegiac emblem of the heroism of the muscular male body. We might note here Joe Gargery in Charles Dickens's *Great Expectations* (1860–61), whose work at the village forge provides a kind of artisanal nobility in contrast to Pip's ill-fated quest to rise above his class and to lead a life of unmanly leisure as a gentleman. For an industrializing nineteenth-century America, Henry Wadsworth Longfellow wrote in 1841 the popular beloved poem "The Village Blacksmith" extolling the muscular craftsman whose body takes on the strength of the new iron machines:

Under a spreading chestnut-tree
The village smithy stands;
The smith, a mighty man is he,
With large and sinewy hands;
And the muscles of his brawny arms
Are strong as iron bands.

His hair is crisp, and black, and long,
His face is like the tan;
His brow is wet with honest sweat,
He earns what're he can,
And looks the whole world in the face,
For he owes not any man.[21]

Informed by this sense of manliness lost with the rise of machine production, reformers in England and America sought to resurrect handwork. In late nineteenth-century England and America, the Arts and Crafts movement sought to reestablish the craft system of the workshop. William Morris, an English disciple of Ruskin, set up a workshop and commercial company, Morris & Co., to produce handmade objects. Elbert Hubbard formed a similar group called the Roycrofters in East Aurora, New York. These experiments did provide creative labor for men as well as women in producing such items as handprinted fabrics, books printed on a hand-press, and handpainted china. As lovely as these objects are (fabrics made from Morris designs are still sold), problems emerged in the effort to revive craftsmanship. For one, the laborious skilled and semiskilled work made the goods expensive, more so than mass-produced commodities, and thus available only to a wealthy clientele. Furthermore, as in the workshops of classical and medieval times, much of the creative design work gravitated to the master, Morris or Hubbard, with the often repetitive stages of production carried out by lower-level assistants. And yet, these arts and crafts projects for all their inherent contradictions must be valued for seeking alternative forms of craftsmanlike labor and self-worth for workers in the age of industrial capitalism.

But to focus on the decline of hand labor is to overlook the continued linking of masculine identity with skill in the machine age. For if we move beyond the narrow equation of craft with handwork to see craft more generally as *technē*, as activity requiring long training leading to expertise, then mechanization provides new modes of craft. As the hand-weaver, the architectural sculptor, and the wood-carver vanished, a new elite of men emerged whose craft lay in operating the machine. In the new railways of the 1840s, the locomotive drivers, engineers in our terminology, performed a skilled craft in distinction to the laborers who laid the tracks. The men who operated the power-looms in the nineteenth-century textile mills formed a labor elite compared to those who merely watched the machines or carried bales of cotton or finished cloth. The operators of steam-powered cranes and steam hammers for driving piles mastered a new form of *technē*. These skilled craftsmen of the industrial world often saw themselves as an elite renewing the medieval handicraft guilds. In the 1860s in America, locomotive drivers forming a labor union called themselves the Brotherhood of Locomotive Engineers.

The Craftsman Today

If we define craft narrowly as work of the skilled hand, then surely with the rise of the machine a man's identity as craftsman became marginalized.

And today weaving or throwing pots carries a touch of the unmanly in not participating in the aggressive and competitive activity of business. For many men, practicing handicraft assumes a secondary place in shaping and maintaining the self. Making things with their hands is for many men not an occupation but a hobby. Woodworking in the basement or refitting the house on weekends often serves as psychological compensation for what seems inauthentic labor working up sales or tracking financial data on a computer screen.

But we can expand the definition of craft as *technē*, as practice rather than theorizing, to include skilled work in the material and technology of our own time. In this enlarged view, the contemporary craftsman employs an expertise that fuses the hand with the mind: scientific knowledge with the skill of the body in the material and immaterial world we have created. As in the early factories, some practices cannot be automated. The crane operators on construction sites today are experts who have mastered their machines. The auto mechanic has acquired knowledge of gears and of electronics as with greasy hands he applies this knowledge to the often unique qualities of each misfiring engine. The electrician must know about circuits and current flows, but in his practice he must pull wire through walls and ceilings and install switches in individual situations by the strength and dexterity of hand and arm. In a profession accorded higher status, surgeons—neurosurgeons, urologists, and plastic surgeons—have learned about nerves and synapses and skin; but in the final analysis, their work depends on the skill of their hands in excising tumors or opening blocked passages.

If craft persists in the handling of contemporary technology, yet in other areas the valorization of technical expertise has diminished. The contemporary artist does not, and here I generalize, see himself as a craftsman. In contrast to the Middle Ages, there is no guild of artists. The trajectory of the artistic career no longer demands acquiring technical expertise in the atelier of a master artist but now draws upon the romantic ideal of individual inspiration. We now have boy geniuses in art. Paintings and sculpture are admired less for their skill in representation than for their newness of conception. Indeed, some forms of art, such as conceptual art, have eliminated entirely the shaping of material into significant forms.

Yet, even if artists no longer arise through the system of training epitomized in the medieval guild system, apprenticeship as the acquisition of occupational manhood through lengthy hands-on training by a master continues a vigorous life in preparing what we can define broadly as the craftsmen in the modern world. To be a neurosurgeon requires absorbing book learning in medical school and then after, a general internship preparing for one's specialty by working under an established brain surgeon in the operating room. Here he (or she) is given more and more responsibility from opening up and closing the skull to operating on the brain itself, all under the eye of the master surgeon. Finally, the surgeon in training himself becomes a master working with his team on the brain while training a new generation of apprentices.

The system of apprenticeship applies also to more traditional crafts. It is worth quoting at some length from the account offered by Plumbers Union #1 of the training of plumbers in contemporary New York City to see the continuity between the classical world and the present in shaping young men into craftsmen. For plumbers as for physicians, New York State, much like medieval cities, has turned over training and certification to what can best be seen as the modern guild of plumbers. The plumbers union quite self-consciously sees itself as continuing the ancient craft tradition in using the traditional system of apprenticeship, journeyman, and master.

> Apprentice training in Plumbers Local Union No. 1 is not just a "job." It is a structured learning system that leads to a career. The education and experience received by an apprentice plumber is lifelong training for a career in the Plumbing Industry. This has been our tradition and it has continued to thrive, grow, and expand over time. In ancient times apprenticeship was known in relation to indentured servitude and the gradual exchange of knowledge from Master to Apprentice. This relationship and informal training continued into the modern era in the skilled trades.
> . . . The education and experience received by an Apprentice Plumber is lifelong training for a career in the Plumbing Industry. Plumbing is an ancient, yet modern craft. Time tested methods of plumbing are combined with the science and innovation of the modern technological world.[22]

The union also provides continuing education for those at the journeyman stage who, in the age of invention, must keep abreast of technological changes, in contrast to the emphasis on the continuity of tradition in the classical and medieval world:

> As technology, equipment and codes continue to change in the plumbing service industry, you need to keep up with the most up-to-date procedures on the job. The Plumbers Local 1 Training Center has a qualified staff of journeymen instructors to help you get the job done effectively and efficiently.

For Mechanical Equipment and Service journeymen who want to keep up to date on the latest materials, methods, products and codes, the Plumbers Local 1 Training Center offers a variety of service journeyman training courses.[23]

For the plumber, as for the electrician and the surgeon, masculine identity—a sense of being a man—is validated by society. Like the status of master bestowed by the guild, the medical license as neurosurgeon is awarded by the other masters in the profession, as is the status of master plumber or master electrician. Internally, identity is achieved by commitment to the code of performing competent skilled work—removing the tumor, turning the lights back on, stopping the leaks, or repairing the engine. Shoddy work, pipes that will soon leak, roofs that drip, tumors that return all violate the code of the occupation and vitiate the sense of self. Identity in craftsmanship, then, stands vividly in contrast in our time to the hegemonic definition of manliness as judged by wealth.

Thus, even with mechanization of production and the shift of reality to the computer screen, the tradition of the craftsman persists. The skilled practice of hard-won skill, competence, and ethical integrity judged by peers, and fellow craftsmen continues. And even if our legacy from the Greeks of prizing the abstract and the theoretical over the concrete and material persists, as in the denigration of vocational training in our educational system, surgeons and plumbers, crane operators, and electricians still take on their identity and their manliness from the practice of *technē*. Hephaestus was lame, but he was also a god.

Chapter 4

Economic Man and the Rise of the Middle Class

In the late eighteenth century and into the nineteenth, there emerged in Europe and in America a system of mechanized manufacturing within an economic regime of industrial capitalism. This industrial and economic revolution brought into being a new form of manliness—middle-class economic man.

As the industrial revolution gathered force, the power of the hereditary aristocracy whose wealth was based on agricultural production declined. This landed aristocracy had maintained a vestigial sense of Athenian manliness in a life devoted not to labor for monetary gain, but to honorable obligation to serve the king and state as warriors and as public servants. But as the wealth generated by manufacturing increased, social power shifted to a new class: to men of commerce and to the owners of the new factories. Within this new world of industrial capitalism, the identity of these men no longer derived from martial valor nor, as with the Athenians, from the duties of public service.

Man was redefined as "economic man." Manliness as service to the common good in war and in peace was replaced by an ethos grounded not in community but in individual self-interest motivated by rational calculation of economic gain. For both the owners of the factories and its workers, manliness was performed through working hard, making money, and accumulating the commodities so easily produced by the machine. This radical shift in the criteria of manliness, so seemingly natural to us today, was justified by a Protestant theology that spiritualized commercial success as a sign of being chosen by God.

For both the middle class and to a certain extent the working class, manliness was linked to ambition taking place by competition with other men that was judged by the acquisition of money. The worth of a man was now defined by his productive ability in a commercial and industrial world. Within a system devoted to productivity, in contrast to a shame society that valued honor, the personal life of men was shaped by a new ethos often termed "middle-class morality," which also guided the respectable working class. At the center of this ethos was restraint in behavior so as to avoid a wasteful expense of a distinctly male energy that could best be utilized in industrial work. Such moderation extended to one's sexual life. Gone was the predatory sexuality of the warrior or the polymorphous sexuality of the Athenian citizen. Instead, the man of business and the industrial worker were bound by compulsory heterosexuality and compulsory marriage within which they took on the role of breadwinner for the family. This control of the self was symbolized by a radical shift in male costume, from the flamboyant dress of the warrior to the dark suit that to this day marks the successful businessman.

Mechanization and the Protestant Ethic, the Reshaping of Masculinity

The rise of industrial capitalism in the West and its attendant transformation of manliness depended on the interlocking of two distinct systems—the technological system of mechanization and the theological system of Protestant ethic or the work ethic. Together these shaped a new masculine identity. Let us take these systems separately, keeping in mind they are intertwined and mutually supporting.

The Rise of the Machine

The rise of industrial capitalism, the system under which we still live, depended on a set of interlocking inventions that emerged in the later eighteenth century in England and continued with increasing momentum across Europe and America into the nineteenth.[1] The central innovation of the industrial revolution was the development in the late eighteenth century of the steam engine, the device that by heating water to its boiling point in a contained space generated the expansive power of steam. The power of steam was applied in many ways. First came the stationary steam engine that by the late eighteenth century turned the iron machines of textile mills that cleaned, spun, and wove cotton. Then arrived the steam engine on wheels, the locomotive that by the early 1830s pulled passengers and freight along rails at hitherto unattainable speeds. There appeared, too, such devices as the steam hammer whose powerful blows could drive piles for buildings and bridges as well as beat molten iron into girders or guns.

For our purposes, we can see the steam engine shaping masculinity as well as shaping iron. At its core, the industrial revolution substituted mechanical power for wind and animal power. People were no longer transported in stagecoaches by horses; grain was no longer ground in mills powered by wind sails or falling water. Crucially for the history of manliness, the steam engine also substituted mechanical power for the power of men's muscles. This substitution of mechanical power for muscular power restructured masculinity by devaluing the ancient definition of manliness that valued the muscle power of the male body. The valor, worth, and very identity of the ancient warrior and the medieval knight depended on the strength of his good right arm that could power his sword or spear so as to cleave through armor. An important element of Athenian manliness was what we now call a good body, a ripped torso displayed in the *Discobolus*[2] that was both an aesthetic and sexualized value as well as a preparation for the duty of war. The craftsman, too, notably the blacksmith and the armorer, as apotheosized in the lame Hephaestus, was defined by his upper-body strength at the forge. But with the rise of the machine, in foundries large pieces of metal for rails, beams for buildings, standardized locomotive elements, and girders for bridges were forged by the steam hammer. Transportation was no longer by sails hauled into place but by steamships. And wars were not fought in face-to-face combat with sword and spears but over a long distance by repeating rifles and iron cannons.

As we have discussed, mechanization sent to the margins the identity of man as craftsman. For machines could now produce with greater accuracy and greater efficiency than by hand the goods formerly made by crafts—nails, barrels, shoes, furniture, and silver tableware. Even the most complex skills could be imitated. The Victorians invented wood-carving machines, silverplating machines, and machines to weave complex patterns into cloth. We see in our own world the remnants of such crafts and trades in occupations like the carpenter, the worker in high steel, the electrician, and the plumber. But most manufacturing involves guiding increasingly robotic devices, and most men work in service rather than in the making of objects. Deskilling of men became the goal of efficient industry. With the skill of the hand no longer needed in production, the craftsman became instead a tender of machines.

The Protestant Work Ethic

Industrialization as a process of technological innovation cannot be separated from the web of attitudes and values generally termed the work ethic or the Protestant ethic, which in the West supported this revolution and set technological change within the structure of free-market capitalism. Whether industrial capitalism generated the Protestant ethic as its spiritual justification or whether the Protestant ethic generated industrial capitalism is a nice but irresolvable historical question. It is best to say that the theological and the technological are inextricably interconnected and mutually reinforcing in creating the identity of middle-class economic man.

The work ethic emerged from the doctrines of Calvinism, a denomination of Protestantism. According to the teaching of John Calvin, a Swiss Protestant minister (1509–64), individual salvation was gained neither by maintaining faith nor by good works but by a mysterious process of election by God. The question arises then of how these secular saints are to be recognized in the world. The answer, which of course fit in well with the activity of the emerging commercial society, was that the elect were marked by worldly success in business attained by hard work and frugality. Thus, committed labor with its resulting commercial achievement became a sign of being chosen by God.

This Protestant ethic marked a radical reversal of biblical teaching as to the relationship of manhood to wealth. Jesus preached, "It is easier for a camel to go through the eye of a needle than for a rich man to enter into the kingdom of God" (Matthew 19:24). From the early Christian era through the Middle Ages, the highest reach of holiness for a man was to take a vow of poverty and retreat from the world into the priestly celibacy of the monastery. But in the industrial era, it is riches that mark a man as the chosen of God and His servant in the world. Not the regime of poverty, but the lust for wealth marks a man as a man. And in many forms of contemporary religion or religiosity, especially in America, faith is still is seen as the path to riches, and the successful man is seen as somehow one of the divinely chosen.

This Protestant ethic also subsumes what we now call the work ethic in another extraordinary reversal by industrial society of ancient teaching as to the relation of work to manliness. Scriptural doctrine was turned on its head. In Genesis, work in the Garden of Eden appears easy and pleasurable, but when Adam commits the sin of disobedience to God, he and Eve are expelled from this paradise. Work now becomes for Adam, and by extension for all men, a curse: "In the sweat of thy face shalt thou eat bread, till thou return unto the ground; for out of it wast thou taken: for dust thou [art], and unto dust shalt thou return" (Genesis 3:19). In the Bible, then, necessary daily labor for survival is a blight upon human life: the price paid for defying God. And for an agricultural people in a dry climate, labor as punishment drew force from the contrast with an imagined life of easeful work in an ever flourishing lush garden that needed little cultivation.

As we have seen, in other preindustrial societies, physical work, for the craftsman as well as for the manual laborer, was considered a lower form of manliness or even unmanly. Work was associated with slaves and with women who spun and wove clothing at home. Warriors lived only for fighting; between battles there was only training and leisure, sex and feasting. Achilles was not a builder; the samurai did neither construction nor crafts. The armor of warriors was made for them by lesser men; Hephaestus made the shield of Achilles. In Athens, slaves under the guidance of the builder lifted and shaped the marble of the Parthenon. Indeed, the highest achievement of Athenian manliness depended on the labor by slaves that enabled physical and mental self-development, aesthetic contemplation, and philosophical discussion. The elite Athenian citizen, as we have seen, looked down upon on the *banausoi* of the city-state as practicing work with the hand rather than with the mind and spirit. In the view of the Athenian elite, handwork narrowed rather than expanded male consciousness and deformed the male body, and as such was closer to the occupation of a slave rather than a citizen.

Why then was the labor with the sweat of the face and in the workshop revalued from a sign of sinfulness or slavery to a sign of near-divinity. How was work transformed from curse to blessing? How did the site of manliness shift from the battlefield or leisured self-development to the factory and the countinghouse? How then did a man become a man through the performance of hard work?

Again, we can think of how the values and actions that define manliness emerge from the needs of the social system. In a world of warring tribes, as in the age of Homer, warriors are essential. In classical Athens, the practice of disinterested service within a participatory democracy demanded men of comprehensive thought and oratorical skill. Similarly, for an industrial society, dedication to work, even exhausting and unsatisfying labor in mechanized factories, is essential for economic growth as measured by production. Within the expanding industrial capitalism, then, the work ethic came to dominate middle-class male consciousness. Consistent effort became the sign of true manliness. Even today, men take pride in spending long hours at the office and on the road.

Furthermore, society called upon men to see work, as physically debilitating and psychologically unfulfilling as it may be, as generating a spiritualized masculine identity. Listen to Thomas Carlyle in 1843, the influential Victorian prophet of the early factory era in England, calling on industrialists and industrial workers to see factory labor as fulfilling a God-given imperative that he called "The Gospel of Work." In high biblical rhetoric, Carlyle preached that labor in the mills was the path to the mental well-being that defined the new economic man:

> A man perfects himself by working. Foul jungles are cleared away, fair seed-fields rise instead, and stately cities; and withal the man himself first ceases to be a jungle and foul unwholesome desert thereby. Consider how, even in the meanest sorts of Labour, the whole soul of a man is composed into a kind of real harmony, the instant he sets himself to work! Doubt, Desire, Sorrow, Remorse, Indignation, Despair itself, all these like hell-dogs lie beleaguering the soul of the poor dayworker, as of every man. But he bends himself with free valour against this task, and all these are stilled, all these shrink murmuring far off into their caves. The man is now a man.[3]

In the industrializing England of the nineteenth century, poets and artists justified the ethic of work by heroicizing the powerful male body of the laborer as manifesting a high form of manliness just as, paradoxically, such muscularity was being replaced by the machine. In an extremely popular painting called *Work* (1852–63), the Victorian artist Ford Madox Brown created a deeply emblematic yet realist painting to symbolize the work ethic. The canvas shows a group of navvies, the British term for construction workers, digging a ditch in the London suburb of Hampstead.[4] Here the daylight highlights the forearms and bare chest of the working-class diggers endowing their muscles with the divinity that according to the Protestant ethic is manifested in such worldly effort. In the background, the haughty wealthy man on horseback is in the company of a woman rather than, like the workers, within a community of men. Not working himself, the rich man registers a disdain for the navvies and exhibits a leisure that has now come to exemplify effeminacy. At the sideline, watching but not digging is Thomas Carlyle himself, with hat and beard, the Victorian prophet of the doctrine of work showing his appreciation of labor. To rationalize the contradiction between observing and not getting your hands dirty, the artist described Carlyle here as a "brain worker."[5]

In addition to validating industrial labor itself, the new association of work with manliness justified the shifts of social power that industrialization brought. Before the rise of the machine, wealth and power in England and in Europe lay with the aristocracy whose income came from inherited agricultural land that they rented to tenant farmers. This landed aristocracy did not work. Indeed, commerce, or what in England was termed *trade*, was incompatible with aristocratic manliness. Their fields planted and harvested by their tenant farmers; their own lives followed the traditions that the landed aristocracy saw as coming down to them from classical Athens. They hunted, entertained other aristocrats, traveled, and collected art. And like the Athenians, many engaged in public service, as officers in the army or members of Parliament.

With the rise of the factory system, power and wealth now derived from industry rather than agriculture. Manliness has always been configured to justify social power, and so the signs of manliness shifted to the activities of the industrialist. As manliness became associated with work and with monetary success, the manly style of aristocratic life devoted to physical and mental self-development for its own sake, as exemplified in ancient Athens and passed down through the study of classical literature at Oxford and Cambridge, came to be redefined as unmanliness, as effeminacy. Thus the centuries-old connection of manliness with bodily grace and with intellectual and aesthetic cultivation was broken. The hereditary aristocrats were now seen as idle dilettantes. The successful economic man became the new aristocract. Carlyle speaks of "The Working Aristocracy; Mill-owners, Manufacturers, Commanders of Working Men."[6]

And yet, distinct and differing forms of manliness exist simultaneously in all societies. In England, especially, the aristocratic class devoted to leisure as well as public service continued to flourish and command positions of political power to this day. In England from the nineteenth century to the present, as industrialists as well as rock stars such as Mick Jagger become wealthy, they imitate the manly style not of the work ethic, but of the British aristocracy, often buying large country houses from impoverished landed aristocrats. Indeed, this desire to employ monetary success to inhabit a preindustrial style can be seen as one of the reasons for England's industrial decline since the early nineteenth century.

It should also be noted that the work ethic took hold much more strongly in America than in England and Europe. In America, with the exception of Southern slave owners on their plantations supported by the labor of chattel slaves, there was no significant landed aristocracy to provide an alternative form of manliness to compete with the identity of economic man. The truly American man is the hard-working man. Yet, paradoxically, American men work so they do not have to work. Hard work is seen as a means to a life of ease. The man who has made his fortune in his web start-up is envied and yet also disdained in another one of the many contradictions that mark American manhood. The ethic of work still sits uneasily in our definition of manliness.

Finally, it might be said that the masculine identity of the warrior was now displaced into commercial activity. Warriors engaged in battle as a competition to the death with honor and reputation as the goal. Now the commercial sphere became the theater of war, finance a battlefield. The essence of the new capitalism was competition by the individual against other individuals. For economic man, the struggle sought a new form of honor and reputation measured in monetary wealth. And the manly skills demanded in the commercial battle of manliness resonated with those of Achilles—boldness, expertise, selfishness, pride, and the intense desire to win.

Radical Individualism: Economic Man as Economic Unit

Within this mutually reinforcing dynamic of theological doctrine, secular belief, and technological change, men were reenvisioned as individuals, isolated atoms within society driven by rational economic self-interest. In short, man as warrior or citizen or craftsman gave way to a new man: economic man. This redefinition of masculine identity sees the ideal man within a capitalist society as an essentially self-regarding individual looking only to his own personal well-being: a well-being defined solely in monetary terms.

This equation of manliness with radical individualism is very recent, only several centuries old, yet this definition of man and his motivation has captured contemporary consciousness. The radicality of this shift in the definition of manliness becomes clear if we look back to the precapitalist, preindustrial communal meaning of manhood. Before industrial capitalism, in general, self-worth derived in large measure from participation in the society. The warrior derives his sense of self from his own personal achievement in battle as he also participates in a larger totality of other warriors and of the tribe or state. The *Iliad* turns on Achilles moving from a private petulance as he sulks in his tent to his fighting both for revenge and for the Greek cause. The elite Athenian prides himself on his own self-development, but such physical and mental growth is also a means for him to fulfill his identity as a citizen by participating in the *polis* and fighting in the phalanx. A United States Marine takes his sense of self from being irrevocably bonded to other Marines within the Corps.

The medieval craftsman set his own skills within the bonded community of the guild. His masculine identity was in good measure a social identity that drew upon the approval and judgment of other skilled workers. But as handicraft ebbed in the machine age, so did the power of the craft guilds. Within the early industrial system, men, even skilled craftsmen, were transformed into individuals bargaining with factory owners for employment and for wages. In this situation, the labor union movement arose that ideally bound workers into a community, much like the guilds, and that could negotiate wages and hours through strength in numbers. And yet the tensions between the collective idea of the unions and the drive to individual economic effort continue into our own time.

This radical redefinition of man as individual rather than as participant within an all-male community was reinforced by the theological shifts of the Protestant Reformation. For our purposes in charting the history of manliness, a significant element of the Protestant Reformation lay in its break with the universal Catholic Church by replacing institutional authority with independence, substituting for the virtue of obedience the virtue of independent thought. The starkest example lies in the interpretation of the Bible. Whereas the Church saw the interpretation of the Bible as determined only by the Church itself, Martin Luther, leader of the Reformation, preached the need for each person to read the Holy Gospel for himself so as to come to a personal understanding. Furthermore, salvation no longer depended on unquestioning obedience to Church teaching. Even though, as noted earlier, Calvinism believed in the mysterious divine election of a few, for most Protestants salvation depended on the effort of the individual whether in maintaining faith or doing good works or both.

Thus, bolstered by theology and the demands of industrial production, the ideology of radical individualism motivated by self-interest marks contemporary ideology. In the age of industrial capitalism, to be a man, a man must depend not on government or guild but on himself and on his own efforts. In America, the philosopher Ralph Waldo Emerson in his influential essay "Self-Reliance" (1841) employed the metaphor of the newly invented structure of corporate shareholding to limn manhood as the rejection of social norms to achieve individual freedom:

Society everywhere is in conspiracy against the manhood of every one of its members. Society is a joint-stock company, in which the members agree, for the better securing of his bread to each shareholder, to surrender the liberty and culture of the eater. The virtue in most request is conformity. Self-reliance is its aversion. It loves not realities and creators, but names and customs. Whoso would be a man must be a nonconformist.[7]

In 1859, at the height of Britain's industrial development, a man with the suitably optimistic name of Samuel Smiles wrote a colossal best seller called *Self-Help: with Illustrations of Conduct and Perseverance.* This manual for advancement, whose self-help descendents still clog our bookstore shelves, asserted the primacy of self-interested action as the means to self-development.

The spirit of self-help is the root of all genuine growth in the individual; and, exhibited in the lives of many; it constitutes the true source of national vigour and strength . . . all experience serves to prove that the worth and strength of a State depend far less upon the form of its institutions than upon the character of its men. For, and civilization itself is but a question of the personal improvement of the men, women, and children of whom society is composed.[8]

Here Smiles reverses the Athenian ideal of *paideia* in which the full personal development of mind and body is both an end in itself and a means to uphold the participatory democracy of the city-state so eloquently celebrated by Pericles in his "Funeral Oration." Articulating the ethos of personal gain that is still with us he rejects the notion of men taking their self-worth from communal life. Smiles rejects the idea of community entirely: "The nation is only an aggregate of individual conditions."[9] Rather than men improving themselves for the good of the polis, Smiles, in contrast, sees the polis or what he calls "civilization" as existing only for the "personal improvement" of the individual.

As conservative Prime Minister of England Margaret Thatcher was to state in 1987, "You know, there is no such thing as society. There are individual men and women, and there are families. And no government can do anything except through people, and people must look to themselves first. It's our duty to look after ourselves and then, also to look after our neighbour."[10] It is, then, our duty to look after ourselves before we look after our neighbor, and we might note here the moralized term "duty" is now applied to self-interest. To help look after others is secondary, following in priority our first obligation, which is to our own individual well-being.

With the shift of wealth from inherited land to industry, there appeared yet another new masculine identity—the self-made man. As we have noted, before the rise of industrialism in Periclean Athens, as in preindustrial England, the source of wealth was primarily agricultural land passed down by aristocratic families. Such assets supported Pericles's education and political activity. Thus one's social and economic status was fixed; a man was a lord or a peasant, and that standing could not easily be changed. But by the end of the eighteenth century with wealth coming from inventions, innovation, and the establishment of factories, men of ambition could generate wealth for themselves by their own efforts. A man could be self-made; he could fashion himself, make his self. The self-made man became for industrial society an epitome of manliness. The man who merely lived off his inherited wealth or who through lack of ambition remained in the class into which he was born was considered effeminate, not really a man.

With the belief that a man's condition of life was not determined by birth but achieved by ambition and skill, the narrative of manliness took a new form. The ideal trajectory of the life of man in an industrial world plotted him rising from the working class to the middle class, and from the middle class to the wealthy class. From the late eighteenth century to the present, literary tales of manhood chronicled the rise as well as the fall of the self-made man; novels charted the gains and the losses in this quest for economic success. The possibility of social mobility opened up a world of achievement for even the lowest-born male, but with the opportunity of success came the opportunity for failure. Refashioning the self brought its inevitable losses and gains. In the narrative of self-making, the young man from the provinces must go to the city to make his way but in doing so must leave behind his family and communal rural life. As he moves to a higher social class, he necessarily breaks the bonds with his origins. The doctrine of self-reliance necessitates a break with reliance on others; this fracturing of male bonds inevitably brings loneliness and isolation. Zeal for wealth as the mark of manhood leads to a distorted crippled self epitomized in the miserly Scrooge of Charles Dickens's *A Christmas Carol*.[11] A life informed by incessant competition against other men fractures the homosociality that had from ancient times characterized manliness.

The novel, the new literary form that emerged in the late eighteenth century with the rise of industrial capitalism, was dedicated to charting this new economic narrative of a man's life with all its contradictions, its possibilities, and its injuries. Examples of literature of the self-made man abound, but let us consider the common features of two familiar examples—in England, Dickens's *Great Expectations* (1861);[12] and in America, F. Scott Fitzgerald's *The Great Gatsby* (1925).[13]

Each shows a young man fashioning or making himself. Pip, Dickens's protagonist, is an orphan; the novel begins with him as a child vainly trying to decipher the tombstone of his parents. Jay Gatsby has cut himself off from his living father. A working-class boy from the American heartland, he has literally made himself by changing his name to Jay Gatsby from James Gatz. For both Pip and Gatsby, social ambition is inextricably tied to sexual desire for a woman of a higher class. For economic man, even sexual desire is monetized; sex and money are fused. Gatsby aspires for wealth to win the upper-class woman, Daisy, of whom he says, "Her voice is full of money."[14] Pip aches to rise in the world to have the beautiful Estella (star). Each naively believes that wealth and social standing will bring sexual satisfaction.

In both novels, wealth is linked directly or indirectly to criminality suggesting that the single-minded focus of economic man on gaining riches erodes social justice. In *Great Expectations,* Pip's inheritance comes from a convict. Even though the convict, Magwitch, has gained his wealth from hard work in Australia to which he has been wrongly transported, still the taint of the prison house sticks to all those involved in monetary transactions, such as Jaggers, the criminal lawyer. This fusion of crime with money contrasts to the work ethic of Joe, Pip's foster father, the heroic artisan at his rural forge. Gatsby has gained his wealth and fabulous mansion on the North Shore of Long Island by a criminal enterprise suggested to be bootlegging.

Finally, each novel shows the cost of this dreaming by economic man, particularly the destruction wrought by a socially validated selfishness. At the loss of his reputation and wealth, Pip turns from self-interest to unconditional love in attempting to spirit his surrogate father, Magwitch, out of England in order to evade the death penalty to be visited on the convict. From this selfless effort, Pip is born again into the unconditional love found in Joe and his new wife, Biddy. Dickens was of two minds and the writer of two endings as to whether Pip should gain a chastened Estella. But each ending shows Pip leaving the world of competitive self-interest.

The narrative of rising in the world was particularly attractive in America where there was no established hereditary aristocracy. Thus the American Dream. Gatsby never gives up this American dream. But his ideal of upward mobility smashes against the reality of the established order of wealth in America that stifles the aspiration of newcomers like James Gatz. Daisy has married Tom Buchanan, a man from the American aristocracy not of land but of inherited wealth, of old money as opposed to new. And the Buchanans, both Daisy and Tom, conspire in the killing of Gatsby in order to preserve their wealth even at the cost of maintaining their unhappy marriage. Gatsby is found floating dead in the swimming pool of his mansion. At his funeral, only his father, whom he rejected, and his only true friend, Nick Caraway, appear to mourn. Gatsby remained a believer to his end in the American Dream that failed him. Yet the dream continues. In the still-thrilling closure, Nick says, "Gatsby believed in the green light, the orgiastic future that year by year recedes before us. It eluded us then, but that's no matter—tomorrow we will run faster, stretch out our arms farther.... And one fine morning—.So we beat on, boats against the current, borne back ceaselessly into the past."[15]

Middle-Class Morality

The conditions that redefined manhood in the industrial age also transformed the ideals and the practice of male sexuality. Gone was the association of manliness with the predatory virility of warriors epitomized in the squabble of Achilles and Agamemnon over Briseas. Gone, too, was the Athenian homoerotic man-boy relation grounded in admiration of the adolescent male body. Instead, in an industrialized world where the production of commodities and of wealth became the highest priority for men, male erotic desire was channeled to that end. The sexuality of economic man was now governed by the sexual code of middle-class morality.

Manliness was now defined by the imperative of marriage. Although, as we shall see, there were anti-marriage tendencies among nineteenth-century men, in general, for middle-class society the real man was the married man. Certainly in preindustrial times men had married. Hector was married but as his choice to battle Achilles against the pleas of his family demonstrates his self-identity as warrior took precedence over domesticity and moved him to embrace death with honor over familial obligations. The Spartan marriage ceremony mimicked warrior rape; during his adult life, the Spartan husband lived with other citizen-warriors in military barracks. The Athenian citizen married, but his taking on the responsibility of the head of a household of relatives and slaves was but one component, but not the primary one, of his multiple duties as citizen. Although the elite Athenian male often showed affection for his wife, as in the example of Pericles, acting out his homoerotic desire with young boys coexisted along with his connubial duties and seems to have been his primary erotic relation. But from the late eighteenth century and continuing into our own time, men and male sexuality became domesticated. Heterosexual marriage became the center of masculine identity. Within an industrial society the married man was defined by his role of breadwinner supporting his family through hard work. From the early days of the industrial revolution in nineteenth-century England, and as we see in contemporary America, to be unemployed and thus unable to provide food and housing for wife and children was, and continues to be, a deeply unmanning experience.

This historically new imperative for men to become breadwinners within marriage can be seen as a way of binding them to the industrial system. Quite simply, being married with children provides a compelling reason to follow the work ethic. One must labor, no matter what the circumstances, to provide food and shelter for the family. Given the unprecedented association of manliness with marriage, the unmarried man came to be considered unmanly. In the late nineteenth century, the man who does not marry is given the new name of "bachelor." The bachelor, then, becomes socially dangerous since without a family to maintain, he can direct his male sexual energy to pleasure rather than commercial or industrial labor.

The linking of manliness with marriage for the middle and for the respectable working classes depended upon a new conception of marriage itself. Marriage was no longer based on the transfer of property or dependent upon considerations of maintaining aristocratic dynasties. Ideally, marriage was now based on affective attraction, or on love between husband and wife. This form of marriage, termed companionate marriage, quickly became the norm with the exception of the aristocracy who were still guided by dynastic considerations. The married state for men became not only the site of achieved masculine identity but also the center of erotic satisfaction. Furthermore, sexual activity was to serve only for production of children. After all, an industrial society needed workers and consumers. Furthermore, since the nineteenth century believed that sexual energy was the basis of power in men, limiting the expenditure of male sexual energy to reproductive sex within marriage made available a surplus of energy that could be channeled to industrial production.

With this domestication and regulation of male sexual energy, what emerged was a new sexual ethos for men: the ethos of marital fidelity. This middle-class code called for sexual faithfulness to one's wife, in sharp contrast to the historical equation of virility with a predatory, affection-free sexuality that marked the warrior, as in the normative use of slave girls by the Trojans and the Greeks. For the Athenian elite, marriage that included sex with one's wife as well as sex with adolescent boys and female prostitutes seemed the natural way of life for men. Of course, middle-class morality with its insistence on marital fidelity generated, as do all scripts of masculinity, irreconcilable conflicts that came to mark modern male life. The older male ethos of virility continued even as fidelity became the social ideal. With the rise of sexual strictures, the middle class increasingly sought sexual satisfaction outside of marriage. In the nineteenth century, the streets of New York and London surged with prostitutes, and keeping a mistress seemed natural for the seemingly respectable middle-class man.

Furthermore, setting the family as the site of emotional value created another conflict, a schizoid break for middle-class men. Combining the identities of businessman and husband called for two opposing forms of consciousness. Within the Darwinian world of business, men were expected to be hard, ruthless, and self-interested in the battle for wealth so as to be valued by their male peers. If the office was the battleground in which men now proved their manliness to other men, the home was the locus for the softer side of the male psyche. The office was the male sphere; the home was the female sphere. Once within his suburban villa, the businessman and industrialist could be restored from the rigors of combat by the selfless wife and recharged for the daily commercial struggle. When coming home from the office or factory, men had to shift from hard to soft, to being affectionate to his wife and nurturing to his children. To be a middle-class man, then, one had to be both tough and tender, performing with the manly aggressiveness of the warrior in the commercial world, and acting in the home with the compassionate and sensitive feeling traditionally associated with the female.

The centering of emotional life in the home generated a counterreaction that drove men to seek an affective life outside the home, not only with mistresses and prostitutes but also with other men. The constraints of the marriage imperative led, paradoxically, to an anti-marriage movement among men, primarily for the impulse to create or perhaps to recreate the all-male societies of earlier time. The nineteenth century saw the proliferation of men's clubs and secret male societies such as the Moose and the Elks in America and, in England, private clubs that provided a refuge from marriage, domesticity, and wives. In the homosocial world of clubs and societies, men could be men.[16] Although in our contemporary world with women now working as equals within the formerly all-male world of business, the structure of separate spheres has begun to dissolve, yet men still seek all-male sanctuaries where they can congregate with other men, especially to enjoy traditionally manly activities such as hunting, fishing, and sports.

Reconceptualizing the Male Body

This new vision of economic man with its emphasis on productivity was grounded in theories that reconceptualized the male body as a producer or generator of energy. Within an increasingly secular world, this energistic theory of men emerged from new scientific theories, especially thermodynamic models, and with technological change that increasingly saw human beings as machines.[17] Such theories of male bodily energy meshed well with ideas of channeling or, in Freudian terms, sublimating the sexual drive to industrially productive ends.

There emerged in the nineteenth century several ways of conceptualizing this specifically male energy. One of the most delightful notions, and one still with us, is thinking of the male body as functioning in a "spermatic economy" powered by "spermatic energy."[18] This model holds that the source of distinctively male force is located in the sperm or semen generated by men. The spermatic economy, like the monetary economy, is engaged with the production as well as with the expenditure or depletion of this spermatic energy. Any outflow of seminal fluid decreases the store of energy within the body. This view of male ejaculation as a depletion of male energy continues in vestigial form in our time in the question of, for example, whether football players should have intercourse before the big game. Since the creation of semen is limited, the goal of the spermatic economy, and thereby the goal of manly behavior is to regulate the outflow of this precious bodily fluid. Excessive expenditure or unregulated flow is the sign of unmanly behavior since draining this reservoir of male strength attenuates the work ethic. The connection between male sexual activity and middle-class economic manliness is clear. In the nineteenth century, the term for male ejaculation is an economic term; to ejaculate semen is to "spend." Thus, a man can be an unmanly spendthrift using up his vital energy in wasteful sexual activity rather than saving his spermatic energy for productive tasks. We might note here the opposition to earlier valuations of manliness as virility in which manliness is valued by sexual potency judged by the number of sexual encounters.

With this new sense of sexual manliness as sexual thrift, several attributes of manliness within middle-class morality become understandable. In the nineteenth century, masturbation was considered the greatest of unmanly sexual vices since semen was "spent" only for selfish bodily pleasure. What was termed "self-abuse" challenged healthy male sexuality since such selfish spilling of sperm depleted a young man's energy that could be better directed to useful work. Similarly, the famed middle-class puritanism with the imperative that male sex be contained within the marriage, and within marriage to be confined to procreation, again limited the expenditure of spermatic energy. Even the taboo against homosexuality that linked same-sex male sex to unmanliness can be attributed to fear of a male sexual practice that did not lead to reproduction and that spent spermatic energy in pleasure rather than work.

Within the new world of machine technology and of industrial production, there emerged another reconceptualization of the male body as an energy system. Here the source of vital power in men does not lie in the production of spermatic energy. Instead, drawing upon the new science of thermodynamics and the rise of the machine, this theory likens the male body to a motor. Like the steam engines that men work with in the factories, the male body is an engine.[19] Man is a living machine. Like a steam engine, a man burns fuel internally in the form of food rather than coal. As the food is consumed it generates heat and energy that powers the muscles and the mind. The vestiges of such theory remain in our language to describe behavior. For example, like a locomotive, we have to "get up steam" to get going. In a later nineteenth-century variant of man as energy system, the body is perceived as the analogue of the new electric motor since electricity was seen as the vital force powering the human system. Like a motor, a man is filled with an electric charge that powers his movements as a worker.

This theory of the male bodily system as a steam engine or electric motor works well to strengthen the effort to control male behavior within the industrial system. Within the view of man as engine, as well as within the model of spermatic energy, the central issue for industrial work is regulating male energy on the factory floor. Seeing the worker as an engine, the question becomes how to control the motor so as to be most productive. We still speak of a fruitless outburst of energy as "blowing one's stack," a lost allusion to the explosion of steam boilers under pressure. An exploded boiler in a locomotive cannot pull the train; explosive outbursts waste energy for the human engine. Within this energistic model, unregulated mechanized labor could expend so much energy over the long day that the worker becomes exhausted, his energy dissipated, and his production declining. Thus, fatigue because of work that is too hard lowers worker output. For the employer, the regulation of the energy of the worker becomes the chief concern. Pushing the worker too hard will be self-defeating, leading to fatigue and exhaustion. Pushing the worker too little at the machine will cut into profits. Thus the workplace becomes ruled by the regime of efficiency so as to achieve maximum productivity. The worker becomes another engine to be regulated and maintained.

If the male body is a living engine or motor, for middle-class and working-class men, the life outside the factory or office is transformed into a kind of yard where they can regenerate the energy needed for manly labor. To use another vestigial metaphor from the nineteenth century, family life and vacations and handicraft hobbies all serve the utilitarian function of "recharging our batteries." Manliness means avoiding excessive and wasteful spending of energy. Manliness resides in a moderate regulated life. Manliness means living as a husband who husbands his sexual energy within marriage. Above all, manliness now means dedicating energy within the work ethic so as to fulfill the masculine identity of breadwinner.

Chapter 5

I Am a Man: African-American Masculine Identities

During the bitter strike of the sanitation workers of Memphis in 1968, the strike that led to the assassination of Martin Luther King Jr., the African-American employees gathered, each holding a sign reading "I *AM* A MAN."[1] These simple words held up by blacks fighting a white municipal government in the late twentieth century powerfully register that the demand for decent wages and safe working conditions (one of their members had been crushed to death by the compactor mechanism inside a garbage truck) is grounded in the more profound desire of these African-American men to be seen by a dominant white society as men, to be no longer excluded but to be accepted into American manhood. It is this recognition of black men as men that has been denied over the long history of African Americans in the United States.

Enslavement: Three-Fifths a Man

Black men from Africa were first brought as slaves to what became the United States as early as 1619. Gradually, a racialized slavery, that is, an enslavement limited to blacks, was established primarily in the southern colonies but also to a lesser extent in the northern ones, especially in New York State. By the time of the American Revolution, slavery had been written into law. Within the legal system, the offspring of slaves were born into the enslaved condition of the parents so that slavery became a perpetual condition.

With independence, the system that denies manhood to enslaved black men was written into the Constitution, the foundational document of America. In what can be seen as the original sin in the founding of the nation, the Constitution asserts that the American dedication to "life, liberty, and the pursuit of happiness" does not apply to black slaves. In the discussions about basing representation in the House of Representatives on the population, the question arose about how slaves were to be counted. In a compromise, the drafters of the Constitution rejected full manhood for slaves; such persons are to be counted not as a whole man but only as only a fraction of one. The passage is worth quoting: "Representatives and direct Taxes shall be apportioned among the several States which may be included within this Union, according to their respective Numbers, which shall be determined by adding to the whole Number of free Persons, including those bound to Service for a Term of Years, and excluding Indians not taxed, three fifths of all other Persons" (Article 1, sections 2, 3). In America's founding document, then, enslaved black men are not men, but only "three fifths" of a man. Here it should be noted that many of the founding fathers were themselves slaveholders. Thomas Jefferson, the author of the Declaration of Independence, like most slaveholders of the Deep South, fathered children with one of his slaves.

Furthermore, the Constitution concretizes the existing legal system that considered enslaved black men as not men, but merely property owned by white men and under the slaveholders' full control. Based on the legal view of slaves as commodities and strengthened by the American belief in the sacredness of property rights, what were called fugitive slave laws required that even if a slave escaped from bondage in a state where slavery was legal to a state where it had been abolished, the escaped slave was not free but remained the property of the slave owner and could be claimed by him. Property rights in slaves extended across state lines. A fugitive slave had to be returned to his owner. The Constitution asserts the validity of these existing fugitive slave laws: "No Person held to Service or Labour in one State, under the Laws thereof, escaping into another, shall, in Consequence of any Law or Regulation therein, be discharged from such Service or Labour, but shall be delivered up on Claim of the Party to whom such Service or Labour may be due" (Article 4, sections 2, 3).

In the period from independence to the Civil War, the legal status of slavery in the United States varied since it was a matter reserved to the states. Slavery was abolished in most northern states (including New York, New England, and Pennsylvania), continued to be legal in the border states (Delaware, Kentucky, Maryland, West Virginia), but flourished in the states of the Deep South (Virginia, South Carolina, Georgia, Alabama, Mississippi, Louisiana). During these years, slavery in the Deep South became an essential economic institution generated by the need for labor-intensive cultivation of the primary cash crops of tobacco and, particularly, cotton. After the invention by Eli Whitney in 1794 of the cotton gin, a machine that efficiently and cheaply separated seeds from cotton fiber, the southern states increased cotton acreage, thereby increasing the need for slave labor. By the beginning of the Civil War, cotton comprised half of the total exports of the United States. The bales were shipped mostly to the newly mechanized textile mills of England to be spun and woven by the newly industrialized workers. Thus, the economy of what came to be called the "Cotton Kingdom" became dependent on the harsh field labor of enslaved men and women. Even though the slave trade, the importation of people from Africa, had been abolished, the slave population in America grew in the nineteenth century as slave owners found breeding slaves for their labor and for their sale to be a profitable business. The slave population grew from 1.1 million in 1810 to 3.9 million in 1860 with the enslaved population concentrated in the Deep South.

In the South, black men and women were enslaved within a system of chattel slavery, a particularly vicious form of servitude. Within this structure, and it must be emphasized that the components of the system were written into law, a slave is under the total control of his or her owner. The slave is the personal property or chattel of the slaveholder and can be bought and sold as a commodity even if that meant separating husband from wife or parents from children. Chattel slavery allowed the slave owner the full rewards of a slave's work even if the slave is rented out as a craftsman, for example, to another white person. The African-American quest for manhood is essentially a quest to eradicate the effects of chattel slavery.

In its practice in the Deep South, chattel slavery was designed to continue the system by eradicating any trace of manhood in the enslaved black man. As we have seen, in its varied forms, masculine identity depends on both an inner sense of self-worth and the validation of this self-being by society. Chattel servitude aimed at erasing this sense of self. Indeed, it systematically excluded black males from the very category of men.

Knowledge and the means of attaining knowledge about the self and about the society were rigorously withheld from blacks. Literacy for slaves was forbidden by law. A white who taught a black to read faced legal punishment and social ostracism. As Frederick Douglass shows in the opening of his achingly powerful *Narrative of the Life of Frederick Douglass, an American Slave,* the system did not even allow him to know the origins of his being as a man. Even the date of his birth was kept from him: "I have no accurate knowledge of my age, never having seen any authentic record containing it. . . . It is the wish of most masters within my knowledge to keep their slave thus ignorant."[2] Nor was Douglass, nor other slaves, allowed to attain the fullness of self that comes with knowing one's father. And even if the father were known, identity grounded in race would be attenuated since within the world of American slavery the father was often the slave master: "The opinion was also whispered that my master was my father; but of the correctness of this opinion, I know nothing; the means of knowing was withheld from me."[3]

Frederick Douglass was originally named Frederick Augustus Washington Bailey, taking his last name, ironically what is conventionally called the family name, from his mother, Harriet Bailey. With only the matrilineal line known, not knowing the father nor being raised by one set enormous obstacles for a slave establishing his own masculine identity as a father. Furthermore, the role of father did not exist legally for slaves nor did the identity of parent. The identity of a father was particularly tenuous since a man, as property, could be sold at any time, separated from his children and wife, and sold down the river to New Orleans for the profit of his owner. Yet in spite of the potential and arbitrary selling of fathers and mothers, slaves developed a sense of familial survival beyond the nuclear family with children cared for by others in the community in times of trouble.

In the antebellum South, then, the issue for enslaved black men was not only developing a sense of self as a man, but also the radical and profound exclusion in this white-dominated system from the biological category of man per se. Laboring like a mule in the fields, unable to read and write, a commodity to be bought and sold—in the eyes of the slave owners envisioned as engaging only in savage pleasures—the enslaved black within the regime of slavery was seen as, and in many ways reduced to, the category of beast. Douglass, our most articulate and eloquent observer of chattel slavery from the inside, describes a slave auction: "We were all ranked together at the valuation. Men and women, old and young, married and single, were ranked with horses, sheep, and swine. There were horses and men, cattle and women, pigs and children, all holding the same rank in the scale of being."[4]

The Christian slave-owning society may have seen the enslaved blacks as beasts, but then as now, these were fantasies of whites created to justify their oppression of blacks. It must be remembered and emphasized that the intense and severe regimen designed to transform the slave into a beast working the cotton field was a regime upheld by the fear of the lash and that this system simply did not succeed. Rather than eradicating a sense of self within black men, the system gave birth to an intense desire for manhood defined as freedom from white oppression. Oppression generated resistance within the self, manifested in varied forms of rebellion. Slave revolts occurred in spite of the horrific penalties for rebellious slaves. The intense fears by the whites of such rebellion indicates the hidden sense in the slave owners that the field hands were not happy darkies but secretly longed for freedom. Such fears were realized when during the Civil War slaves deserted the plantations with the arrival of Union troops. The zeal for manhood as freedom from white domination intensified as the harshness of the system increased. Douglass recounts an episode in which he fought with a particularly cruel overseer as a way of asserting manhood as freedom from servitude: "This battle with Mr. Covey was the turning-point in my career as a slave. It rekindled the few expiring embers of freedom, and revived within me my own manhood. It recalled the departed self-confidence, and inspired me again with a determination to be free."[5]

Furthermore, the effort to isolate the slaves from the humanizing and broadening effect of culture by forbidding reading and writing efforts failed. Denied the power to read, the slaves of the South developed their own primarily oral culture to provide a communal identity. From this oral culture emerged, for example, the songs of slaves, the spirituals longing for freedom. This oral culture of the antebellum slave world also continued the traditions and tales of West Africa, the homeland from which their ancestors had been so violently taken. Such folktales were adapted to their own situation registering a society dominated but resistant, with a secret culture hidden from the whites. Primary among the figures of such stories—and it is important to note a model for masculine behavior of African Americans after emancipation—is the trickster, a figure in many mythologies and in the American South carried over from the West African Yoruba mythology. The trickster figure uses his wits, his cunning, and secrecy to survive and subvert the more powerful figure, in the way that the enslaved blacks resist white oppression. A well-known African-American trickster is Brer Rabbit who outwits the Bear as a coded symbol for the white man. In one well-known tale, Brer Rabbit, when caught by the Bear, pleads not to be thrown into the briar patch, which Bear does, not realizing that this underbrush is Brer Rabbit's home and sanctuary.[6] From white society, the enslaved blacks adopted Christianity but transformed the Bible to focus on Exodus as the divinely guided escape from slavery rather than the Bible as justification for the enslavement of dark-skinned peoples. Still, vestiges of the African religion of animism continued. Douglass tells that before his fight with the overseer, he consulted with Sandy, an old man respected in the enslaved community who still knew the magic of Africa. Drawing on African tradition, Sandy told Douglass to find a certain root to carry on his right side so that he would always win his battle with the white man. And win the fight he did.[7]

In addition to the rich oral culture developed during enslavement, as slaves escaped from the Deep South and abolitionist sentiment grew in the North in the years before the Civil War, there flourished a powerful African-American literary form—the slave narrative, the genre of autobiography by former slaves relating their experience of slavery, their liberation, and their search for self-identity as free persons. Of the more than eighty of these slave narratives that appeared in the North, the most influential was Frederick Douglass's *Narrative of the Life of Frederick Douglass, an American Slave* from which I have quoted extensively for its perceptive and immediate account of the dehumanizing apparatus of chattel slavery. Antebellum slave narratives also include works by women such as the autobiographical *The History of Mary Prince, a West Indian Slave* (1831) and *Incidents in the Life of a Slave Girl,* by Harriet Jacobs (1861).

The slave narrative, whose form continues in African-American literature into our own time as in *The Autobiography of Malcolm X,* follows a specific trajectory that registers the African-American movement to manhood defined as freedom from white domination. These narratives assert that for black men, the first and necessary step to achieving an identity as a man must be casting off the false consciousness of blacks as inherently bestial and degraded, one that has been imposed by the institution of slavery and by the continued racism after emancipation. What is striking about these slave narratives is their affirmation that personhood as manhood must be achieved by first understanding and then rejecting the systematic program developed by whites to destroy the black self. Indeed, the very act of writing an autobiography that records the development of the self is an assertion that the black is a man and not a beast: a person of consciousness and agency. The ability to write, in itself, proves the existence of an intelligent human self. The title page of Douglass's work asserts "WRITTEN BY HIMSELF" to show, quite simply, that blacks can write without the aid of a white man. Then, too, the description of slavery by a former slave in itself demonstrates successful resistance to the "soul-killing" regime (the phrase is from Douglass) of slavery.[8]

The slave narratives, then, focus on liberation not only as physical escape, but on the liberation of consciousness from the manacles forged by white society to chain the black mind. In each tale there is a moment or continued moments of shedding the false consciousness imposed by slavery through the internal act of standing outside, and thereby understanding, the system. Often adapting a Christian evangelical structure, these autobiographies limn the experience of being born again, born again as a man. And with that distance comes the author's realization that traits exhibited by blacks are not innate but a result of a systematically imposed regimen of dehumanization. This refutation of racial innateness speaks to our time. Douglass describes from his experience the enabling step to black manhood as moving from an unquestioned slave consciousness to a subject position outside that consciousness. He writes of being "myself within the circle: so that I neither saw nor heard as those without might see and hear," then moving to an understanding of that internalized culture of oppression, to "my first glimmering conception of the dehumanizing character of slavery."[9]

The move to African-American manhood comes through refusing and often turning to one's advantage the practices of domination. One method is to take on the forbidden practice of reading. Reading, as learning the history of the West that has created his condition, is to awaken the dormant self of the slave. Douglass describes the power and intent of forbidding literacy by placing himself in the mind of a slave owner who knows that if you teach a slave "how to read, there would be no keeping him. It would forever unfit him to be a slave. He would at once become unmanageable, and of not value to his master."[10]

Another step in becoming a man is through self-naming, a crucial move in fashioning one's self by fashioning one's own ancestry, thereby becoming one's own father in a society that denies knowledge of origins to a person defined as property. After escaping to the North, Douglass feels he must create his own new self by giving himself a name. He tells his Northern white patron that he "must hold on to that [Frederick] to preserve a sense of my identity" since the first name or given name differentiates an individual within a group. But he must create a lineage for himself, since such white ancestry was hidden by the use of his mother's name. His patron "had just been reading the 'Lady of the Lake,' [poem by Sir Walter Scott] and at once suggested that my name be 'Douglass.' From that time until now I have been called 'Frederick Douglass.'"[11] In naming himself after the courageous hero of Scott's poem, this former slave is fashioning his own self, creating an identity of his own that will continue through his emancipated life where he will indeed be known as Frederick Douglass.

It is striking that into our own time, the genre of the slave narrative still charts the steps needed to achieve an African-American masculine identity defined as freedom from white control. Of these contemporary narratives grounded in the slave narrative form, the most influential is the bestselling *The Autobiography of Malcolm X*.[12] For Malcolm X, as for Douglass, the initiating move toward masculine identity lies in comprehending and thereby rejecting what Malcolm X calls throughout the narrative "brainwashing," the process through which whites work to sustain a sense of inferiority in black men. With the perspective of a man freed from the false consciousness imposed by racism, he looks back to his unfree youth: "Mine was the same psychology that makes Negroes even today, though it bothers them down inside, keep letting the white man tell them how much 'progress' they are making. They've heard it so much they've almost gotten brainwashed into believing it—or at least keep accepting it."[13] For Malcolm X, again as for Douglass, entry into black manhood comes with the realization of his own brainwashing that made him as a youth think that being a hustler, drug dealer, and a thief was cool. For a black man, whether legally enslaved or enslaved by racism, becoming a man comes with realizing the enslavement of the mind by white society.

This recognition for Malcolm X, again as for Douglass, comes through reading: a practice forbidden during slavery and a practice ignored by many emancipated African Americans. In these narratives of a man's life, reading becomes a rite of passage into an authentic black manhood. While in prison, Malcolm X on his own inspiration takes on an omnivorous and intense regimen of reading in Western history that by linking himself to the wider scope of the past brings about a conversion experience that allows him to be born again as a man freed from white brainwashing. He realizes that white Christianity "taught the 'Negro' that black was a curse. It taught him to hate everything black, including himself. It taught him that everything white was good, to be admired, respected, and loved. . . . It brainwashed this 'Negro' to always turn the other cheek, and grin, and scrape and bow, and be humble, and to sing, and to pray, and to take whatever was dished out by the devilish white man."[14]

With this internal liberation, the man born as Malcolm Little has transformed himself. He rejects the white Christian world to join the Nation of Islam. He changes his identity by changing the name that was the mark of his unfree identity. Like Douglass he retains his given name, that of the individual, but rejects the surname, traceable back to the slaveholder, that he sees as registering the historical white exploitation of blacks as property.

He explains the use of "X" as the surname given to all new members of the black Nation of Islam as representing the African heritage stolen by whites: "The Muslim's 'X' symbolized the true African family name that he never could know. For me, my 'X' replaced the white slavemaster name of 'Little' which some blue-eyed devil named Little had imposed upon my paternal forebears."[15] For Douglass, the former slave, as for Malcolm X, the former hustler, once the false consciousness of white domination is cast off as signified by the name change, new forms of consciousness, new African-American masculine identities must be forged.

Emancipation and After

As Union troops moved into the Deep South during the Civil War, slaves fled the plantations to enter the Union-occupied territory and freedom. This rush to liberty demolished the comforting myths of the slaveholders, myths that have a striking persistence for white Americans—that the blacks in the fields were happy with their life, that blacks were at best subhumans without the power of choice, and that they preferred being cared for to the autonomy of free men. This rush from enslavement as soon as it was possible convinced President Abraham Lincoln, who had shared the dominant view of blacks as a lesser race, that enslaved blacks deserved freedom. That realization of the humanity of blacks as well as the military necessity of freeing blacks so they could join the Union armies, led Lincoln in 1863 to issue as an executive order the Emancipation Proclamation: "All persons held as slaves within any State or designated part of a State, the people whereof shall then be in rebellion against the United States, shall be then, thenceforward, and forever free." Although the Proclamation only applied to slaves within the Confederacy not yet under Union control and did not apply to slaves in the border states where slavery was still legal, the Emancipation Proclamation deserves its almost sacred place in American history as the first action by the nation to abolish the institution of slavery. Slavery was not finally brought to an end in America until the Thirteenth Amendment to the Constitution was passed in 1865: "Neither slavery nor involuntary servitude, except as a punishment for crime whereof the party shall have been duly convicted, shall exist within the United States, or any place subject to their jurisdiction."[16]

With the abolition of slavery in the mid-nineteenth century, the issue arose for the nation of transforming the newly free blacks into citizens. By serving in the Union Army, once freed the former slaves had demonstrated their manliness in what one Northerner called "the display of manhood in Negro soldiers."[17] Now they were to be granted the rights of citizens, once held exclusively by white men. Immediately after the war, in the period known as Reconstruction, the victorious North sought to empower the free blacks of the South. The passage of the Fourteenth Amendment in 1868 revising the criteria for voting rights in the states abrogated the infamous three-fifths clause of the Constitution by asserting that population be counted by "whole number of persons," thus finally and legally recognizing the full manhood of black men. The passage of the Fourteenth Amendment in 1868 legally guaranteed the right to vote for all citizens. The Fifteenth Amendment ratified in 1870 specifically guaranteed suffrage for freed slaves: "The right of citizens of the United States to vote shall not be denied or abridged by the United States or by any State on account of race, color, or previous condition of servitude." Blacks now voted and even began to take responsible positions in the government of the South. The North also sought to have black men become American men by making them landowners who would finally be allowed the rights to the fruit of their own labor, a very American ideal. In the words of a Northern general distributing plantation land to the freed slaves, through working their own land the free blacks could achieve a "manly self-dependence."[18]

But by the 1870s there was a strong backlash in the South by the white power structure against the restoration of black manhood and what was seen as black power. As the North lost interest in the situation of the freed blacks, Southern whites began a campaign based on terror by such groups as the Ku Klux Klan to restore white domination. In spite of the Fourteenth and Fifteenth Amendments, threats of violence and new legal restrictions in practice denied the vote to blacks in the South. The land transfer was now construed as land confiscation, and free ownership gave way to the share-cropping system in which blacks once again worked for white landowners. The infamous Jim Crow laws enforced racial segregation in all areas of life from water fountains to public education to public buses. Once again, full manhood was denied black men; in the Deep South, even a grown black man was called "boy," as if blacks could never grow into adult manhood. These laws and social practices were elaborated and enforced in the South from the 1870s until the Supreme Court ruling of 1954 in *Brown v. Board of Education of Topeka* outlawed racial segregation in the public schools. The civil rights movement of the 1960s forced the decline and eventual end of segregation in public spaces, and the Civil Rights Act of 1964 outlawed racial segregation in voting.

Given the effects of enslavement and continuing racism after emancipation, from the seventeenth century to the present for African Americans the ongoing achievement of black manhood becomes at its core the struggle to maintain a sense of self against the pressures of white society to dominate and dehumanize. Such efforts to emancipate and shape the self, to break the manacles both of iron and those of the law have taken a variety of forms from slave rebellions; to escaping to the North; to learning to read; to self-naming; and, in our own time, to the nonviolence of Martin Luther King Jr., and to the advocacy of more direct means by black power movements.

African-American Masculine Identities: Separatism or Assimilation

Consider the variety of masculinities in black men in America in our own time—the bow-tied advocate of the Nation of Islam; the jazz musician; the celebrity movie star; the security guard; the multimillion dollar dunker of the NBA; the hip-hop singer and producer; the ghetto dweller; the suburbanite in his SUV; the CEO of American Express; the corporate lawyer; the civil rights lawyer; the community organizer; the Christian minister; the president of the United States.

Such a list—and the list is hardly inclusive—illustrates that if we can speak of a single masculine identity in the ancient warrior cultures, in the Athenian city-state, and in the nineteenth-century business world, we cannot speak of a unitary African-American masculine identity. The identities are as diverse as the reasons for this multiplicity of black selves. For one, blacks transported to enslavement in America were a people culturally disenfranchised, uprooted from their past, and from the unified culture that grounds all forms of manhood. Furthermore, the enslaved blacks were, by design, excluded from membership as men in the nation in which they resided and worked. By law, blacks were excluded from American citizenship. They were not socialized into a valorized manly role such as the craftsman enjoying the fruit of his labor or the warrior awarded honor by his tribe. Instead, the enslaved black was made into both a commodity and a beast, a living being denied even the basic identity of a human being.

Deprived of a social identity, the freed slaves and black men to this day had to fashion their own personal identities as well as construct a social context and a history that validates a personal sense of self. To generalize, for African-American men the primary issue in shaping group and personal identity is the extent to which they see their being as African or as

American. (Although the term "American" can suggest inclusivity and diversity, in this discussion of African-American identity I am using the term to refer to the hegemonic white middle-class culture of the United States that many African Americans quite accurately see as excluding blacks.) Taken by force from Africa rather than immigrating by choice as did so many from other countries who have become American citizens, the free black faced the choice of whether to assimilate into the dominant white culture or return spiritually and culturally or even physically from the Black Diaspora to his ancestral home. This conflict within African Americans does not exist in each man as a simple dualism, but, as with so many other issues, along an always shifting continuum between the extremes of African and American. African-American manhood, then, is an unstable hybrid existing in a tension between integration and separatism.

Within the separatist model, African Americans see themselves as living within the Black Diaspora. Forcefully removed from their ancestral homeland, they live as exiles in strange lands. African Americans constitute a homogeneous people dispersed through North and South America and the Caribbean. Their true home and authentic identity lie in Africa.

Within the diasporic condition, the project of achieving personal and group identity lies in maintaining and revivifying the connection with the homeland that was so brutally cut off by enslavement and the continuing cultural hegemony of white culture. For many African Americans, the restoration of selfhood means maintaining a sense of their African past, even if this project generates some tension within life in America. We can recall Frederick Douglass reaching out to the shaman Sandy for a magic root to aid in his physical battle for manhood with the overseer and yet not being able to admit that African magic won the battle for him.[19] The thrust of separatism has been to assert black pride, a pride strengthened by restoring to view the achievements of African societies. This effort to create a usable past has been sustained by a new African history that has turned from recording the conquests of white imperialists to describing the accomplishments of the societies from which the slaves were taken. With the emergence of a historiography of Africa freed from a Eurocentric perspective, we now know, for example, of the brilliant sculpture in bronze and wood created in the highly sophisticated kingdoms of West Africa, especially those of the Yoruba people, the ancestors of most of the slaves transported to the United States.

In spite of continued efforts in America to preserve the *Gone with the Wind* myth of the kindly master and mistress in the plantation house and the happy field hands singing in the cotton rows, the history of slavery is also being rewritten to show not only the vicious oppression, but also to resurrect the heroic resistance of slaves. Such retellings of black history are enormously popular both in assuaging white guilt and in fostering black pride. The best-selling historical novel *Roots: The Saga of an American Family* by Alex Haley and the TV series based on the book trace the life of a slave from his transportation from Africa to his resistance as a slave in the Deep South. The author's return to the African village of his own "roots" brought to general awareness the actual origin of African Americans and introduced the term "roots" into common discourse. Other best sellers about the heroism of slaves include *The Beloved* by Toni Morrison. This recuperation of a heroic past means that a black man can choose to draw upon the history of his people to validate his own self-worth. By thinking of himself as an African in America, he can assert a masculine identity as the descendent of a dispossessed but heroic people.

At its most extreme, separatism advocates an actual return to the African homeland. We must remember that identity is often imposed by others. In the nineteenth century, many whites, seeing black slaves living in America as not truly American, sought to expel them from the nation. With a mix of charity and racism, in the 1820s northern white organizations sent freed blacks in a reverse colonization back to Africa to found the nation of Liberia. Like many whites, Abraham Lincoln saw blacks as a lower form of beings, thus not truly American. To resolve the slavery issue, he advocated what was then called colonization. Before the Civil War, he called for buying slaves from their masters (property rights must be preserved) and relocating them to Latin America where they could create independent all-black colonies.[20] To his surprise, most blacks demurred.

As the failure of Lincoln's colonization projects illustrate, most African Americans, for all of their connection to their African heritage have rejected the idea of actually leaving America. Still the return to Africa has continued to appeal to some as a viable path to an authentic identity. In the twentieth century, the voluntary return by blacks to Africa appeared in the movement lead by Jamaican-born Marcus Garvey. An activist for civil rights in America in the 1910s, Garvey came to believe that African Americans could only achieve their freedom by returning to Africa. In 1919 he established the Black Cross Navigation and Trading Company, which purchased two steamships to carry blacks to Africa. But the effort at return failed financially, and large-scale emigration by blacks to Africa died as an ideal. In our own time, some American blacks have moved, or moved back,

to Africa. But this extreme mode of establishing identity by actually returning to live in Africa has not had wide appeal. For all the pride in African
roots, African Americans prefer to inhabit their hybrid identity as African
Americans, people of African descent who live in America.

Like all identities, black identity is a complex mix, and one of the main
strands has been an essentialist belief in what is often termed negritude,
specific qualities that are innate in blacks. Originating in an anti-colonial
political movement in the 1930s of French-speaking colonized people, the
idea of negritude countered the colonialist notion that black people require European rule since they are mentally and psychologically inferior.
Instead, the vision of negritude asserts a vital energy innate in black people
that is superior to the sterile rationality of white men. The notion of negritude as a vivid and vital form of being underlies black pride. Negritude
grounds opposition to integration into what is seen as an emotionally des-
iccated, overly logical, dehumanized white world. Frantz Fanon, an influential black anti-colonial writer from the francophone Caribbean, describes
how the racism he experienced as a physician in France spurred his own
resistance to his culturally imposed ambition to become white. Instead of
professional striving, he wanted to "reclaim my negritude."[21] He finds his
identity as a black man in an essential blackness superior to the corrosive
dehumanization he sees in the white world:

> I made myself the poet of the world. The white man had found a poetry in
> which there was nothing poetic. The soul of the white man was corrupted,
> and, as I was told by a friend who was a teacher in the United States, "The
> presence of the Negroes beside the whites is in a way an insurance policy on
> humanness. When the whites feel that they have become too mechanized,
> they turn to the men of color and ask them for a little human assistance."[22]

This belief that blacks from Africa remain more human, more in touch
with their feelings and their bodies remains foundational to many forms
of black identity and certainly informs the categorization of, and often the
jealousy of, blacks by white society. In the first decade of the twentieth century, for example, like many European artists—Picasso is a chief example—
were inspired by African wooden carvings such as masks. Seen through
Eurocentric eyes, these functional and ritualistic objects displayed a primal
or, in the terms of the time, "primitive" power as manifesting negritude.
The performance of black men in American sports, particularly in basket-
ball and football, is attributed to the innate physical prowess of men of

African descent, rather than to the fact that sports has in America provided one of the few paths to upward mobility available to the impoverished and socially excluded.

Certainly music, black music—blues, jazz, soul, hip-hop—has been one of the primary markers of African-American identity as separate from and in its powerful pulse an expression of negritude superior to white being. The idea of black music as "soul" music suggests for blacks and for whites that it is an expression of an essentialist quality of self rather than a logically constructed aesthetic form. Jazz exists as a particularly powerful expression of black soul and of black experience in America. Today hip-hop expresses one of the many forms of African-American manliness, the masculinity of the urban ghetto. The powerful rhythms, the brilliant rhyming, and syncopation attest to an intense energy. The lyrics praise a consciously anti-white, anti-bourgeois life of violence; of disrespect for women; of crime and prison; of physicality and drugs. These songs present a distinctly black identity in their defiance of middle-class norms. The energy and adrenaline rush of such oppositional life is here transformed into compelling art. And the kings of hip-hop in their over-the-top materialism and sexual prowess set one ideal of masculine identity for black men.

If some African-American masculinities perform a separatism often grounded in black essentialism and connection to African roots, other scripts of African-American manliness emphasize the American in African American. These identities manifest a constructivist mode of fashioning the self to the ideals of the hegemonic middle class and the distinctly white definition of manhood.

On escaping from enslavement in the South, Frederick Douglass moved into the dominant, white manliness of industrial, work-oriented nineteenth-century America. He became in Ralph Waldo Emerson's terms self-reliant, working as a calker in the shipyards of New England, one of the heroic artisans celebrated by Walt Whitman. Always respectable, as a free man Douglass married, raised a family, worshipped as a Christian—all forms of manhood denied to slaves. He adopted the name of a Scottish literary hero. Rather than advocating slave rebellions, he wrote and spoke for the white-led nonviolent Abolitionist movement and was invited by President Lincoln to advise on issues surrounding slavery and emancipation. His autobiography is written in Standard English rather than a black dialect and titled the *Narrative of the Life of . . . an* American *Slave* (emphasis added).

Upon emancipation, Douglass and other free blacks looked to the normative American identity of bourgeois manliness as productive worker, as married breadwinner, and as citizen of a democracy. After the Civil War, rather than a return to Africa, blacks in the South sought a distinctly American manhood of independence and agency within the work ethic. They craved and were given land to work so as to fulfill the America Dream denied to the slave of being able to enjoy the fruits of his labor and thereby become a breadwinner for his family. The freed slaves wanted literacy so as to connect with the Western cultural tradition. They flocked to the free public schools provided for blacks during Reconstruction. They wanted to become informed citizens and, like the citizens of Athens, to vote in and to administer a democratic society. Of course, as we have seen, after Reconstruction dissolved, racism drove the white southerners to wrest from blacks the right to earn a living, to be an independent person, to receive a decent education, to vote.

It must be emphasized that the civil rights movement of the 1960s led by Martin Luther King Jr. called for a new emancipation defined as the opportunity for African Americans to attain a distinctly American manhood. The striking Memphis sanitation workers called for the right to be a man, but to be a man defined in particularly American terms. From its heart the movement called for the opportunity long denied blacks to enter the mainstream of American manhood, to be considered a full man rather than three-fifths of a man. Indeed, the strategy of nonviolent civil disobedience counted on the moral return of white Americans to the founding principles of the nation, to the promise of the Declaration of Independence that "all men are created equal." Primarily, the movement sought to secure the right to vote guaranteed in law by the Fifteenth Amendment but denied in practice in the South. This effort assumed that poor black sharecroppers had the ability to enter the identity we recall from classical Athens, with manhood defined by participation in democracy. Such a leap from man as de facto slave to citizen illuminates the faith that these African Americans held in the initial promise of America. This democratic manhood as a citizen, as voter, government official, and legislator that had been realized during Reconstruction was to be once again instituted in America. After intense opposition that lingers in American politics to this day, the Voting Rights Act of 1965 was passed through which the federal government outlawed practices, such as the literacy test, that were used to deny the vote to black people: "No voting qualification or prerequisite to voting, or standard, practice, or procedure shall be imposed or applied by any State or political subdivision to deny or abridge the right of any citizen of the United States to vote on account of race or color." Since the Voting Rights Act, there has been a notable increase in the political power of black voting and in the number of black representatives, senators, and governors. And, of course, as I write there is an African-American president of the United States.

Of course, not everyone in the black liberation movement shared King's belief that nonviolence would succeed by activating the originating moral principles of America and allow blacks into white American society. For some, change based on separatism rather than integration became the guiding strategy. These activists shunned the moral exempla of sitting in at lunch counters and riding interstate buses in the South. Instead, advocates of black power looked to the threat of and even the practice of violent resistance as the means to counter the white racist violence of America. Such extreme groups as the Black Panthers took to posing with guns and even using them against white power. Black power and the threat of violence against racism marked this form of black manhood in America. Black men could become men by throwing off the emasculating effect of subordination. Black manhood in America was to emulate Africans in their wars of colonial liberation in such places as Kenya. The wars of Africa had destroyed colonial rule and through the cathartic effect of violence made men of former colonial subjects.

Malcolm X did not trust white men, "white devils" as he termed them. The Nation of Islam looked to separatism rather than integration into white culture, to black power rather than dependence on the moralized generosity of whites. As a contemporary African-American critic writes, Malcolm X showed that "being black didn't mean being conquered. Black nationalism was black macho. The image that Malcolm X projected held the promise of retaliatory power."[23] Malcolm X urged blacks to cast off the "brainwashing" that continuously regenerated the sense of inferiority in African Americans. In its place, Malcolm X looked to a distinctly hybrid form of black identity. The Nation of Islam, in theory at least, placed a high value on the family stability of middle-class culture, albeit with an emphasis on the subordinate position of women, as a way of breaking with the diminution of the black man as father and the instability of the family that had continued in black culture since slavery. The Nation of Islam also looked to create in blacks the internal self-fashioning of bourgeois life—moral self-discipline in sexual practice, modesty in dress, and rigorous self-control of aggression. And the Black Muslims also looked to the middle-class ideal of economic striving and monetary success as the markers of freedom, although wealth was to be achieved in a separate system of black enterprise rather than by joining the white business community.

Rather than being forced to function within a separate system with liberalization of racial attitudes and the help of affirmative action, black men have been enabled to enter the domain of hegemonic America manhood by performing as economic agents and breadwinners for a stable family. African Americans now attend elite universities. And with education has come economic success for many blacks, even within corporate America. African-American men have become the heads of major corporations such as American Express, Aetna Insurance, Merck Pharmaceuticals, and Citigroup. Here again, Barack Obama is the model of attending Ivy League universities; having a stable family life; and becoming a law professor, senator, then president. And with this economic rise has come the move of many African Americans from the urban ghetto to the middle-class and upper middle-class suburbs.

But the move of blacks from the city to the suburbs manifests yet another tension in the identity of black men in America. In seeking and in achieving middle-class manliness, black men severed their identification with their African heritage and with the ghetto communities in which many such men grew up. Rather than basing their identity on negritude or black community, these men often saw themselves as self-made men (see chapter 4) and grounded their new sense of self in the bourgeois manliness of deferred gratification, rationality, heterosexual sex confined within marriage, and obedience to civil law.

But those left behind in the urban ghetto either through choice or circumstance did not or could not enter this hegemonic American manliness. For many black men in America, the path to the middle class was blocked by a myriad of obstacles, chief among them simple racism. For generations, unions and employers have excluded blacks from skilled labor positions, universities from admission, and professional societies from the practice of law and medicine. Denied access to education leads to low wage jobs or unemployment. Residential segregation in continuing in practice if not in law isolates African-American men in the ghetto. To the inequality in wealth between whites and blacks has been added an inequality in wealth among blacks. Many black men are born into and live in conditions that offer little chance of escape from a cultural and economic world that in many ways replicates the conditions of slavery.

Post-Racial America; Post-Black America

With the election of Barack Obama as president, it seemed to some that America had finally become a post-racial society—that race would no longer become the measure of self-identification, group identification, and external categorization. But some questions emerge about whether, given its foundational racism, America can transcend skin color as the basis of identity.

For one, it is noteworthy that Obama's "race" is a hybrid matter and that such hybridity might exemplify the dissolution of the corrosive dualism of black/white, African/American. As we all know, Obama is the child of an African (Kenyan) father and a white American mother. As such, he is what is now termed, still employing the conventional racial categories, as mixed race. Here we must note, too, the persistence of the America racist idea generally called the "one drop of blood rule." If a person has one drop of black "blood" that person is defined as black. Clearly the converse of one drop of "white blood" as defining racial identity does not apply. Here we might note, too, that Obama is not unique in his racial hybridity. There are, perhaps, few "pure" black persons in America. After all, Frederick Douglass had a white father as did so many enslaved males. Malcolm X repudiated his white ancestry by changing his original surname of "Little" to "X." As mixed or interracial marriages increase in America (laws against interracial marriages or what was termed miscegenation were not judged unconstitutional until the decision of the Supreme Court in *Loving v Virginia* in 1967), the category of race may gradually disappear and the dualism of black/white become anachronistic.

And with the increase in mixed marriages and the recognition of mixed racial origins, identity as African American in any form has become, and will continue to become, increasingly a matter of choice, a matter of volitional self-identification. In his moving and eloquent autobiography, *Dreams from My Father,* Barack Obama tells that as a light-skinned person he could have "passed" as white, particularly since he was raised by his white mother and white grandparents after his father abandoned him. But in an identity crisis in college, he read Malcolm X, and in spite of deep reservations, "Malcolm X's autobiography seemed to offer something different. His repeated acts of self-creation spoke to me."[24] Imbued also with the writings of Martin Luther King Jr., Obama finally self-identified as an African American, moving to Chicago to work in the ghetto as a community organizer after Harvard Law School, marrying a black woman, and establishing himself within the black community and a black church.

A post-racial or post-black America would mean the disappearance of race-based masculine identity. The election of a self-identified black man with a Muslim middle name may appear to exemplify the passage to a nation where the identity of a man is not judged by skin color. As Orlando

Paterson notes in his review of *Who's Afraid of Post-Blackness* by Touré, "Post-blackness entails a different perspective from earlier generations; one that takes for granted what they [African Americans] fought for: equal rights, integration, middle-class status, affirmative action."[25] He notes that such gains have enabled "a liberating pursuit of individuality" for African Americans, but that in America, race still shapes identity, albeit in new ways.[26] The many successful African Americans interviewed for Touré's book agreed that "post-black identity . . . resides in the need to live with and transcend new and subtle but pervasive forms of racism. 'Post-black' does not mean 'post-racial.' The new racism is invisible and unknowable, always lurking in the shadows, the secret decisions of whites resulting in lost opportunities blacks never knew about or even thought possible."[27]

Chapter 6

Jewish-American Masculine Identities

To discuss Jewish-American masculinities in the present, we have to go to the past—to the first century CE. At that time, the religious life of the Israelites was centered on the Second Temple in Jerusalem, the destination of their pilgrimage, and the single site of observances such as animal sacrifices performed by a hereditary priesthood. In 66 CE, the Jews rebelled against the Roman rule that was suppressing their practice of religion. After bitter fighting, Jerusalem was conquered by Roman forces in 70 CE and the Temple destroyed. With the ruin of the place of worship and the displacement of the priesthood, the Jewish people gradually moved to a new, decentralized form of worship and community—Rabbinic Judaism—which enabled the survival of the people to the present day and from which emerged a distinctive formation of masculine identity.

Rabbinic Judaism

Within Rabbinic Judaism, worship was no longer confined to a single location. Instead, individual places of worship, synagogues, were established whose sacredness was bestowed by the presence of the holy script, the scroll of the Torah. Rather than such rites as animal sacrifice, the focus of worship now became the communal reading of the sacred text of Judaism. In place of the hereditary priesthood, leadership of the community devolved to a rabbi, a man chosen for his learning in the Torah and in the interpretation of the law based on the Torah by which Jews lived.

I shall discuss the effects of Rabbinic Judaism on the construction of Jewish manliness in a moment, but a bit more history is in order. With the destruction of the Second Temple and with an oppressive Roman rule that sought to eradicate the Jewish people in what Jews still call the Holy Land, some Jews continued to live there, as demonstrated by archeological evidence of synagogues throughout the land. But most Jews moved from their former homeland to found communities throughout the known world—in Rome itself, in Spain, in what is now the Rhineland of Germany, and in Arab lands—in what is known as the Jewish Diaspora. This diasporic movement continued for centuries as Jews moved throughout the world, especially to Eastern Europe from where, in the nineteenth and early twentieth centuries, they traveled in large numbers to the New World.

It was the conditions of the Jewish Diaspora, especially the severe restrictions imposed on Jews by the peoples among whom they lived, combined with the religious structure of Rabbinic Judaism that generated the specific nature of diasporic Jewish manliness. Given these circumstances and in order to survive as a people, Jews adopted a form of manliness that was the very opposite of hegemonic Western manhood. If we focus on Europe, we see that Jews were allowed to live among Christians but always separated from them. Confined to specific areas with tight restrictions on their movements and occupations, Jews had to turn inward. They were restricted to clearly demarcated urban areas that came to be called ghettos, a term derived from an island in Venice called *Ghetto Nuova,* where the Jewish inhabitants of Venice were forced to move in 1516. Jews could conduct business outside the ghetto of Venice as in other ghettos but had to wear distinguishing clothing. In the eighteenth century, the numerous Jews living in Russia were relocated forcibly to the Pale of Settlement encompassing parts of what are now Russia, Ukraine, Latvia, and Lithuania. Here, Jews lived in small wholly Jewish villages called shtetls or in ghettos in urban centers such as Warsaw or Odessa. But whether in the urban ghetto or the shtetl, the Jews lived a life centered on family and worship separate from the larger gentile community. These Jewish spaces were generally governed by their own Jewish administrations. Jews were, then, not considered citizens of the nations or territories in which they lived. They were not allowed to be Russians or Venetians. Thus, Jews of the Diaspora could not participate in the Western masculine identity of citizen within the civil society. Jews lived as outsiders, participating as citizens only of their own isolated communities.

Of equal bearing on the construction of diasporic Jewish masculinity were the restrictions on occupations that Jews could follow. Since Jews were excluded from civil society, they could not serve in the army and thus could not take on the identity of warrior. Nor did diasporic Jews look to military power of their own in, for example, Jewish militias or self-defense forces as a way of protecting themselves against what was the overwhelming military and police power of the states in which they lived in sufferance. In general,

Jews were limited in entering the role of craftsman. And although some Jews prospered as artisans, they were not granted membership in the craft guilds. In general, Jews were restricted to the lowest and dirtiest of manual occupations such as tanning, collecting scrap, tailoring, and peddling old clothes—occupations that Jews were to continue upon arriving in America. Confined to urban ghettos and Jewish villages, Jews were not allowed to own land; thus the traditional manly role of the farmer was also denied to them. As we shall see, this diasporic exclusion from traditional manly roles was countered by the Zionist ideals of a resurgent Israel as an agricultural society defending itself by force against its enemies.

With the masculine identities of citizen, warrior, craftsman, and farmer denied, Jews were allowed to enter the world of business and commerce only in restricted ways that were useful to the Christian society. Because of Christian strictures against usury, lending money at interest–the necessary work of a commercial society—was to a great extent given to Jews. As Shakespeare's *Merchant of Venice* registers, though accepted in practice, money-lending and its practitioners were employed by and yet reviled by Christian society. Yet Jews prospered in money lending on both a small scale and a large scale, especially in international banking where they could draw on networks of trusted Jewish bankers throughout Europe and the Middle East that had been created by the Diaspora. International Jewish banking houses grew and prospered. Such enterprises as the House of Rothschild that began as a family firm in Germany in the eighteenth century expanded throughout that world. At the local level in such places as Poland and Russia, Jews were useful to gentile society in serving as middlemen between the Christian nobility and the peasants—often running taverns, flour mills, or small shops where they were positioned to incur the anger of the peasants and thus deflect that rage from the nobility.

Banned from the hegemonic manliness of warrior, citizen, or farmer, and allowed to practice only forms of business that positioned them as social outcasts, a distinctive form of manhood was forged in these isolated and oppressed communities. Denied access to the physical manliness of the soldier or farmer, Jewish men inhabited a manhood that defined itself by its difference from the manliness of Western tradition. Jewish masculinity reversed the traditional equation of manliness with muscularity in equating manliness with intellectuality. As noted, the leader of the diasporic community was the rabbi, granted his position because of his ability to read and interpret the law, as well as to affirm the moral values of the biblical prophetic tradition. This rabbinic ideal became the touchstone for Jewish men.

The highest calling for men became the study of the law; the most valued of men was not the breadwinner but the scholar who spent time in study of the Torah and of the interpretive literature called the Talmud. The highest honor for a woman was to marry such a man, even though that meant that since the scholar or eternal student did not work in a trade or craft, the wife had to keep the household going. We can see the equation of manhood with intellect in the well-known Jewish rite of passage for men, the bar mitzvah. Rather than killing an animal or producing a masterwork to prove to other men his right to enter manhood, at the age of thirteen, the Jewish boy becomes a man by demonstrating his intellectual ability through reading in the synagogue service the week's passage from the Hebrew Torah and providing a commentary. Strikingly, then, in contrast to the surrounding communities, the Jewish world was one of universal male literacy.

The normative sexual practice of Jewish men also defined itself by contrast to Western ideals of virility. Rather than the predatory sexual acts that defined the warrior or the multiple sexual encounters both heterosexual and homosexual of the Athenian, Jewish male sexuality was to be kept strictly within the community, within marriage, and devoted to continuing the survival of the Jewish people. Sex with non-Jewish women was unthinkable; marriage with gentiles was forbidden by Jewish law. Jewish male sexuality, then, was by necessity defined by the need to reproduce so as to maintain the population of the community and to prevent the dissolution of the Jewish people through intermarriage. For a Jewish man to be a bachelor was shameful. Marrying a Jewish woman and raising a large family were the signifiers of manhood. Within traditional Jewish marriage, sex was to be devoted to reproduction, as we can see in the numerous children of Orthodox families today. Homosexual acts were strictly forbidden.[1]

From its beginnings, in the effort to distance itself from its origins in Judaism early Christianity defined the sexual drive in men as the origin of sin, indeed as the very source of evil. Within Christianity, celibacy became a virtue for men, the highest exemplar of manliness. The priesthood became an order of celibate men. Judaism holds no such sense of sexual desire and sexual activity as evil. Celibacy in men is neither a virtue nor the mark of a higher form of sacred manhood. There is no tradition that rabbis be celibate. Rather, it is expected that rabbis marry and have children—the more the better. In Jewish tradition, sex is properly imbued with sacredness, a pleasure experienced through the innate desire granted by God. But sex, as noted, must be practiced within marriage, working within the commandment to be fruitful and multiply so as to continue the Jewish people.

Indeed, some Orthodox Jews view marital sex as a mitzvah, a righteous act, to be engaged in on the Sabbath.

Thus, the fusion of Rabbinic Judaism with the restrictions of diasporic life in Europe created a mode of manliness defined by its contrast with hegemonic Western masculinity. Indeed, it can be argued that it was this very difference between Jewish and Western manliness that strengthened Jewish masculine identity for this oppositional manhood was informed by the urgency of maintaining a distinctive sense of self and community as a bulwark against assimilation into the dominant society. Excluded from the roles of warrior or citizen, the diasporic Jew, especially in the urban ghettos and Jewish villages of Eastern Europe, formed communities that valued intellectuality rather than physicality; eschewed martial violence even for protection of the community; practiced a rich sexuality within Jewish law; engaged in international finance and local commerce; and worshipped through traditional observances. There is within Jewish tradition a Yiddish word that defines such manliness. A real man is a "mensch," the term of high praise for a man who is morally responsible, committed to his work, to his religion, to his family, and to the Jewish community. It was this distinctive mode of manliness that Jews brought to America and that accounted for the relative success as well the deep tensions that define the lives of Jewish-American men.

America, the Golden Land: Tradition vs. Assimilation

In 1790, President George Washington visited the Touro Synagogue in Newport, Rhode Island, a congregation of Sephardic Jews, Jews who had come to America from Spain and Portugal usually by way of South America. After the visit he was sent a letter from the congregation asking if the religious freedom of the new nation applied to Jews. Washington replied in a letter to the congregation in eloquent words that still resonate:

> For happily the Government of the United States, which gives to bigotry no sanction, to persecution no assistance, requires only that they who live under its protection should demean themselves as good citizens, in giving it on all occasions their effectual support. . . . May the children of the Stock of Abraham, who dwell in this land, continue to merit and enjoy the good will of the other Inhabitants; while every one shall sit in safety under his own vine and fig tree, and there shall be none to make him afraid.[2]

In these eloquent words, at its beginning the government of the United States affirmed that the words of the Declaration of Independence and the

Constitution applied to Jews. In contrast to Europe, America affirmed full civic and religious liberty for Jews and, most importantly, defined "the children of the Stock of Abraham, who dwell in this land" as full "citizens," as persons freed from the anti-Semitic restrictions imposed in Europe. In this new land, Jews could inhabit fully the identity of citizens of the civic polity. Jewish-American men could vote, participate in government, and enter into any occupation without restriction. For Jews of the Diaspora suffering persecution in Europe and in the Pale of Settlement, America was truly, as it came to be known, "the golden land."

Jews arrived in America in several waves of immigration. They were present in America from the beginning. There are records of Jews living in New Amsterdam. These first Jewish Americans were Sephardic Jews; by independence, synagogues of Sephardic Jews had been established in cities along the Eastern Seaboard, in New York City and, as noted, in Newport, Rhode Island.

The next wave of Jewish immigrants arrived from Germany in the years 1830–70. These German-speaking Jews were shaped by the movement called the Jewish Enlightenment. In Germany many restrictions on Jews had been lifted, and Jews were allowed in many ways to enter the secular society. With the Enlightenment, many Jews had abandoned traditional communities and developed the form of Rabbinic Judaism known as Reform Judaism, which employed the vernacular language rather than Hebrew. Abandoning the distinct Jewish clothing, such as the skull cap, and observances such as keeping kosher, Reform Judaism used Western-influenced liturgical music in synagogues modeled on Christian or Byzantine forms. Yet, these Jews left Germany because of constraints on business and pervasive anti-Semitism. Relatively secular in their style of living, generally middle class, educated, skilled in business, and holding liberal political ideas, the German-speaking Jews did not seek to establish a separate presence but rather easily assimilated into American Protestant society. They brought with them their business experience, often becoming quite successful. They came to establish and own major department stores such as Macy's, bought by the Straus family in 1895; Levi Strauss invented the copper-riveted jeans in the 1870s in California, the origin of Levis; and Hart, Schaffner and Marx was founded by German Jews in 1887. With their financial connections and experience, in nineteenth-century America German Jews established large and successful banking houses such as Kuhn, Loeb and Lehman Brothers. Many German Jews eagerly accepted the new role of citizen within the civil society. In New York State, to take just one example, Herbert H. Lehman, a member of the banking family, served as governor from 1933–42 and U.S. senator from 1950–57. Jacob Javits served as senator representing New York from 1957 to 1981.

The German Jews, then, who arrived in the mid-nineteenth century easily fit into hegemonic America masculinity with their devotion to business, their secularity, their eagerness to enter civil life, their bourgeois respectability, their urgent desire not to be different in their lives, and their very modest and muted religiosity. But in the late nineteenth century, a new wave of Jews, quite different in identity, surged into the United States.

Beginning in the 1880s in the Jewish Pale of Settlement, a horrific series of pogroms (killing of Jews) took place as Jews became scapegoats within the political turmoil of the time. Fearful for their lives and afraid of being drafted for a virtual lifetime of service in the Russian army, Jews streamed from Russia to America, the golden land. From the 1880s to the early 1920s, several million Eastern European Jews landed in the United States, settling mostly in major cities such as New York, Philadelphia, and Chicago. Caught between the power of Jewish tradition and the attractions of American life, these Eastern European Jews, unlike the German-speaking ones, struggled to form a stable Jewish-American identity. I will focus on the issues of the Ashkenazi, as these Eastern European Jews are called, and the descendents of these newcomers since it is the tensions of this group made visible in popular Jewish-American literature and film that often come to mind when we consider the issues of Jewish-American manliness.

The Eastern European Jews who immigrated to America at the end of the nineteenth and early twentieth centuries came directly from the isolated, tradition-bound worlds of the rural shtetls and the urban ghettos of Kiev, Odessa, and Warsaw. In America, Ashkenazi men faced a conflict of identity. Dressed in their traditional black clothing, observing Orthodox religious practices, without secular knowledge, knowing only the sacred texts and Jewish law, and without practical skills, this first generation of immigrant Jewish men faced the secular, rapacious commercial world of America with its religious freedom as well, and we must be blunt here, as its sexual freedom. For the first generation and for succeeding ones of Jewish-American men (and I note again, I am focusing on the Ashkenazi here) identity was characterized not by stability, as in earlier codes of manhood, but by instability, inner conflict. An oppositional stance to hegemonic masculinity preserved Jewishness in the European diaspora. In America such clinging to tradition prevented men from seizing the opportunities offered by the freedom of the diaspora in America. The American way of life, especially in business and the professions, offered outlets for the pent-up intellectual energies of diasporic Jews, and yet such mobility often clashed with the identities forged under the societal restrictions that had shaped Jewish manliness.

Still holding to the culture of the ghettos of Europe, the first generation of immigrant Jews crowded into new ghettos such as the Lower East Side of New York. Here men and women, were often forced into low-wage labor in the overcrowded, unsanitary, unheated, and unventilated sweatshops of the clothing trade. In the garment trade, some Jews, however, challenged the American tradition of individualism and free-market capitalism. Drawing upon the biblical moral tradition and on the sense of responsibility to the community, as well as on the European socialism that had penetrated the urban ghettos of the Pale, men and women worked diligently to organize workers, especially textile workers, into unions that fought for decent wages, hours, and working conditions. Eastern European Jews became leaders in the Socialist movement in America. Socialism for a number of reasons did not take root in the United States, but the association of Jews with progressive movements, such as civil rights, has continued. And even though with their success and wealth, some Jews have moved toward the Right, still a secularized moralism grounded in the prophetic biblical tradition of social justice has persisted within Jewish-American masculine identity.

Even though forced into taxing and exploited labor, the Eastern European Jews had brought with them from the shtetl and the ghetto the equation of manliness with intellectuality and a universal male literacy. As with other traits, this devotion to learning inscribed culturally through the Orthodox yeshivas (religious schools) of Jewish Eastern Europe was in America turned to secular purposes—but not without some tension. Should the Jewish boy in the new land become a rabbi as he would in the old or find new secular possibilities for intellect? Not without Jewish guilt, most Jewish men opted for the secular. There were obstacles of covert anti-Semitism in place that hindered upward mobility. Anti-Semitic feeling kept Jews from the upper reaches of established banking. The gateways to success—elite private universities such as Yale and Princeton as well as medical schools and law schools—had strict Jewish quotas, kept in place until at least the 1950s. Public universities had no such restrictions, and such institutions as City College of New York became a site for learning-hungry Jewish students. In spite of restrictions, the scholarly energy now channeled to secular goals found an outlet in intellectual achievement for Jewish Americans in such fields as medicine, law, science, and the academic world. Here we can cite as examples such figures as Jonas Salk, developer of the polio vaccine; Louis Brandeis, first Jewish justice of the U.S. Supreme Court; Steven Weinberg, Nobel Laureate in theoretical physics; and Lionel Trilling, noted literary critic and influential professor at Columbia. The Jewish masculine identity of intellectuality flourished in secular America.

What is less well known is that on coming to America, many Jewish boys and men rejected this traditional Jewish intellectuality for the physicality of America life, especially in sports. Playing professional sports and losing the self in sports fandom provided a way of rejecting the Jewish heritage of the pallid student. The true American was the athlete, and Jewish males coveted this identity. Sports in America had always been one of the few areas open to new immigrants. The early days of Jewish immigration have come to be known as the golden age of Jewish boxing. Slugging another man into unconsciousness surely redefines Jewish identity. Such boxers as Benny Leonard (Benjamin Leiner), lightweight boxing champion; Barney Ross (Dov-Ber Rasofsky), lightweight, junior welterweight, and welterweight champion; and "Slapsie Maxie" Rosenblum, successful boxer and later film actor became the heroes of the Jewish community for exhibiting a physical toughness in Jews that proved their Americanness.

And as with other immigrant groups, men of the early generations turned to crime, again a kind of refutation of traditional Judaism, even though Jewish gangsters had flourished in the urban areas of the Pale, as described by Isaac Babel in his tales of the Jewish gangs of Odessa.[3] The 1920s and 1930s in America were the golden age of Jewish boxers and also of Jewish gangsters. In these decades and after, a Jewish Mafia often collaborated with the Italian mafia. Murder Inc. often called the Brownsville Boys (named after a Brooklyn Jewish neighborhood) killed both for the Jewish and Italian crime organizations. Their notable or one might say notorious hit men included such Jews as Harry "Pittsburgh Phil" Strauss and Martin "Bugsy" Goldstein. Perhaps the best-known Jewish gangsters were Meyer Lansky (Maier Suchowljansky) and Bugsy Siegel. Lansky worked closely in his early years with the Italian mafia in bootlegging and protection, then turned to establishing mob controlled gambling in Florida, Cuba, and Las Vegas. He had his partner in Las Vegas, Bugsy Siegel, killed on suspicion of cheating him. Lansky is best known to American audiences as the original of Hyman Roth in *Godfather II,* brilliantly played by Lee Strasberg, who discusses the spoils of gambling in Cuba with Al Pacino.[4]

But sport and crime were only stages in the developing masculine identity of Jewish men in America, rather than continuing elements of Jewish-American masculinity. Many Jews easily entered the very American role of the entrepreneurial man of business. As noted, excluded from politics, the military, and farming in the Pale, Jews became tradesmen, often middlemen between the nobility and the peasants. This experience of retail commerce found an opening in an America devoted to buying and selling within a free enterprise economy. Jewish entrepreneurial energy, tuned in the European Diaspora, turned at first to shopkeeping. From beginnings often as traveling peddlers traversing America, including the American West, Jews opened dry goods stores in small towns; these stores often grew to large department stores. Department store names such as Hecht, Hutzler, Wannamaker, and Magnin indicate their Jewish origins. From origins in the garment industry—the rag trade as it was called—some deployed the entrepreneurial energy brought from Europe to follow the American dream, to rise in the world, to create their own companies, as, for example, Ralph Lauren (Ralph Lifshitz), Kenneth Cole, Marc Jacobs, Calvin Klein, and Isaac Mizrahi.

With success in business, Jewish men eagerly adopted the American identity of the breadwinner achieving manhood by supporting his family. Indeed, devotion to family, a dominant trait of the confined diasporic community, coincided with the dominant American middle-class ideal of manhood as supporting a familial domestic life. And as Jews prospered, they rejected the diasporic condition of living in a confined Jewish space, such as the Lower East Side of New York. With prosperity came a move to other areas of the city, then to the suburbs. But there were covert and also overt constraints on residential assimilation, such as marking some communities as "restricted," off limits to Jews. And a vestigial sense of Jewish community, of wanting to live with other Jews, still lingered. Thus, Jewish Americans often moved from impoverished Jewish ghettos to affluent Jewish suburbs, still living with other Jews.

As bourgeois as the stereotypical Jewish-American man may be, as seen in the pervasive image of the Jew as family man, such middle-class identity generated tensions in sexuality for Jewish men. As we have noted (chapter 4), bourgeois manhood set compulsory marriage and the restriction of sexual activity to within marriage as signs of manliness. Such bourgeois regulation of sex nicely coincided with the Jewish diasporic tradition of equating marriage with manhood. But for Jewish men, the prescription of marriage came with the supplemental mandate that it must be within the Jewish faith; marriage to a non-Jewish woman was cause for expulsion from the Jewish community since the children would not be considered Jewish. In America, as Jewish men entered the mainstream society, opportunities arose for sex and even marriage with gentile women. Indeed, given the lure of the forbidden, Jewish men were often attracted to gentile women. For Jewish-American men, the tension between tradition and assimilation was often acted out in sexual terms. Should a man marry a gentile woman and thus be ostracized by the community or settle down with a Jewish girl so as to remain a Jew? Rabbis do not perform marriages between Jews and gentiles. This sexual conflict pervades Jewish-American literature, as in the early stories of Philip Roth in *Goodbye Columbus*[5]; in Jewish-American films, such as *Annie Hall;* and the private life of the stereotypical sexually neurotic Jewish man, Woody Allen.

Jewish tradition in regard to sexuality for men has been hostile not only to intermarriage as a danger to the survival of the Jewish people, but also to homosexuality, perhaps for similar reasons. In the discussion of homosexual identity (chapter 7), we note the severe strictures in the Hebrew Bible against male same-sex relations: "Thou shalt not lie with mankind, as with womankind: it is an abomination" (Leviticus 18:22). In America, male-male sexual relations certainly existed among Jewish men, but, as in the general society, in secret. But with the gay liberation movement and an increasing acceptance of gay life and even of same-sex marriage in the larger community, the question arose for Jewish men as to whether gay identity was compatible with Jewish identity. Can one be a gay Jewish man? As I write, the Jewish community in America is sharply divided. The Orthodox community strictly forbids same-sex marriage and sees the practice of male homosexuality as a violation of divine law. The Conservative branch is deeply split on performing same-sex marriages, whereas the Reform community generally accepts homosexuality and generally blesses same-sex marriages between Jewish men.

The temptations of intermarriage, of gay identity, of residing outside Jewish communities all manifest the most basic identity issue for Jewish-American men—whether to reject personal identification as a Jew. If America offered Jewish men opportunity in crime and sports, as well as in finance, law, and medicine, such freedom also offered the opportunity not to be a Jew, to renounce entirely one's birth and heritage—whatever the internalized guilt that decision may bring. A free society with its possibility of assimilation for Jewish Americans allows the option of just being an American and not being a Jew. America is the land of self-fashioning for men through self-naming. James Gatz can become Jay Gatsby; Frederick Augustus Washington Bailey named after his slave master can become Frederick Douglass; Malcolm Little became Malcolm X. So Dov-Ber Rasofsky can become Barney Ross the boxer; and Ralph Lifshitz can become Ralph Lauren, purveyor and epitome of anglophile preppy style. Renouncing one's identity as a Jew may bring isolation from the Jewish community into which one was born, but escaping from Jewish identity entirely, even in contemporary America, is still problematic. As much as a Jew may reject his heritage and change his name, that the non-Jewish community may still categorize that person as a Jew presents yet another difficulty for Jewish-American men.

In America, then, as Jewish men are increasingly accepted into the larger world in spite of lingering anti-Semitism, the question of whether to inhabit a Jewish identity becomes primarily a matter of choice. Thus, we now often speak of a person not as being a Jew, but as "Jewish identified" in the sense of having made a personal decision about accepting the Jewish identity into which he was born.

Orthodox Jews, Tough Jews; the Variety of Jewish Masculinities

To close this section, I would emphasize again that I have been focusing on only one group of Jewish men living in America—the populous and visible descendents of Eastern European Jews. These Ashkenazi have, in general, achieved middle-class status, entered into the hegemonic America identity of businessman, breadwinner, and professional man; and crowd the popular culture of literature and film. But, of course, there are multiple forms of Judaism and of Jewish masculinity in America. I will here mention briefly Jewish Orthodoxy with its own criteria of manliness and the resurgence of the tough Jew as a challenge to bourgeois Jewish manliness.

The move of American Jews from tradition has not been complete and has indeed generated a counterreaction, a growing movement toward Orthodoxy. The Orthodox world takes various forms. There are the deeply Orthodox sects of Hasidic Jews, such as the Lubavitch and the Satmar, who continue to live in separate communities. These communities descend from the remnants of Orthodox communities that escaped the Holocaust, came to America, and grew and flourished within their closed worlds. These Hasidic Jews, as they are called in recognition of their mystical practice and devotion to a charismatic rabbi, basically reject modernity and the styles of modern American manhood. They preserve tradition by refusing to change. As in the Old Country, the men wear black clothes and white shirts; keep their long earlocks; ideally devote time to study of sacred texts and, in theory at least, follow strict Jewish laws of sexual practice, particularly in raising large families. Yet even these strictly Orthodox Jews exist in tension with American forms of manliness. They drive cars and often have their own retail businesses catering to the general public in such areas as electronics. They dominate the diamond business here and abroad where, as in the earlier days of the Diaspora, a network of trusted Jews throughout the world provides assurance of honesty and craftsmanship.

In America, Orthodoxy, too, has its modulations as it engages American life. The Modern Orthodox movement blends tradition with modernity. The Modern Orthodox do not choose to live separately under the direction of a religious leader. The men are often clean shaven and wear modern dress although always with a yarmulke (skullcap). They work in the professions such as law and medicine and in real estate and finance, along with gentiles. Yet they also are observant. They keep kosher, marry within the faith, and insist on modest dress for women. Young men are educated in religious schools, but in contrast to the Hasidic yeshivas, these schools, such as Yeshiva University in New York City, combine religious and secular studies.

Finally, as an example how for Jews, as for all peoples, the scripts and the ideals of manly behavior are malleable—constantly shaped and reshaped—according to the needs of the society, we will consider the rise of the tough Jew, physical, aggressive, emulating manliness in the surrounding society.

The formation of the Jew as tough guy grew from the Zionist movement that emerged in Europe at the end of the nineteenth century. This movement began as a response to continued persecution of Jews in Russia, and especially to the Dreyfus affair in France in the 1890s, when a Jewish officer in the French army, Alfred Dreyfus, was convicted and sentenced to Devil's Island on evidence that was forged by anti-Semitic French officers. In the nineteenth-century European context, Zionism was one of a multitude of nationalist movements looking to establish a homeland for their ethnic groups. In terms of Jewish history, Zionism looked to assure Jewish survival through establishing or reestablishing a Jewish homeland through the return of the diasporic Jews to what was then Palestine.

The settlement of European Jews in Palestine both before and after World War II, the creation of the state of Israel in 1948, and the continuing conflict of Jewish Israelis with the Palestinians are, of course, still contentious matters. But for our purposes, the important point is that the Zionist movement advocating the settlement of Jews in Palestine and the culture of contemporary Israeli Jews emerging from Zionism are grounded in the redefinition of Jewish manliness. Specifically, the creation of a Jewish state was seen as inseparable from the creation of a new Jewish man through what was termed the "normalization" of Jewish masculinity. Rejecting the diasporic Judaism that fashioned what was seen as the physically stunted, passive, psychologically deformed, unmanly man epitomized in the pale, stooped, soft, perpetual yeshiva student, Zionism called for adopting, for Jewish men, the hegemonic Western masculinity denied to diasporic Jews. With disdain for the diasporic Jews left behind, the early Jewish settlers established in Palestine an agricultural society of Jewish farmers who valued physicality rather than intellectuality. Surrounded by Arab enemies, these first settlers rejected nonviolent passivity for an active militarism. And rather than centering life on religion, these men were determinedly secular, maintaining an ethnic rather than a religious Jewish identification. The image of the ideal pioneer was the muscular farmer, plow in one hand, rifle in the other. The apparent passivity with which the Jews of Europe went to their deaths in the Holocaust only intensified this Israeli turn to a martial masculinity. Surrounded by Arab nations and movements devoted to the destruction of Israel, the compulsion to adopt toughness toward enemies increased. The new Jewish motto became "Never Again." And the Israeli Defense Forces, a citizen-army in the mode of Athens, is renowned, if not notorious, for its discipline and harshness.

Formations of manliness, then, are never stable. New constructions of manhood emerge as social needs shift. Still, ideals of manliness require a usable past. Post-diasporic Israeli society has reached back to elements of Jewish tradition and biblical history to validate and shape its new definition of Jewish manliness. The militarism of Israel invokes the fierce militarism of the Israelites in their conquest of Canaan under Joshua, the ideals of David shown in Israelite imperialism, and the armed revolt against the Romans in which on the peak of Masada Jews, like the samurai, chose suicide rather than capture. Israelis are sworn into the Israeli Defense Force at the summit of Masada declaring "Masada shall not fall again." As we move to the conclusion of this survey of styles of manliness, we see in this Jewish society a return to the beginnings. Israeli Jews, often to the admiration of American Jews, have adopted one of the most ancient forms of masculine identity in embracing the code and practice of the warrior.

Chapter 7

Same-Sex Desire and Masculine Identity

Same-sex male erotic desire and sexual relations have been, and continue to be, constants in society. And these same-sex erotics have been, and continue to be, central to a society's definition of manliness.

In thinking about the role of same-sex desire in the formation of masculinities, we must keep a number of issues in mind. First, the place of such erotics in cultures varies widely. Then, given the universality of such desire, the focus of inquiry must be not simply the question of whether male-male sex is permitted or banned, but rather the form that same-sex Eros takes, particularly the degree to which such sexuality is employed to differentiate the manly from the unmanly. To take one example of the identification of same-sex Eros with manliness—as we have seen, the Athenian elite saw the erotic desire of adult men for beautiful adolescent boys as natural and universal. Yet to be manly in the eyes of other Athenian citizens, adults had to perform these man-boy relations within a courtship code that honored the independence of both the adult and the young man. In doing so, these erotics served as rites of passage into this patriarchal democracy. In contrast to classical Athens, in contemporary America many associate same-sex desire with the unmanly, with the feminine and the effete. Men who practice male-male sex are set as exemplars of the unmanly man against whom true American manliness is defined.

Thus far, in considering the relation of male same-sex desire to the varied social definitions of manliness, I have been careful not to use the word "homosexual." I have done so since we must think about desire between men in the long view of history in which the term homosexual is a recent invention. After all, it would not only be anachronistic but foolish to ask if Achilles and Patroclus or Socrates and Alcibiades or the Spartan warriors were all gay. The idea of the homosexual as an identity for men was simply not present in the classical world. Crucially, as we shall see, the term homosexual as well as the term heterosexual as categories of identity for men were invented in the late nineteenth century in Europe within a great paradigm shift in the definition of masculinity that, for the first time in history, imagined the totality of the male self as determined by sexual object choice: that is, by whether sexual desire was directed to the same sex or the opposite sex. We must realize that the most common questions now asked of a man, "Is he straight?" or "Is he gay?" are of recent origin in the history of masculine identities.

Same-Sex Erotics and Man as Warrior

Since contemporary America is so quick to associate desire between men with the unmanly, it might be best to begin with some reminders of the ancient historical association between male-male desire and the unassailably manly identity of the warrior.

As I write, the United States has finally resolved a long debate at the highest government levels about whether men of homoerotic inclination should be allowed to serve in the armed forces. (The issue has applied to women as well, but given the purpose of this volume, I will focus on men.) Against strong objection by some in the military and in Congress, one compromise solution to this issue, the so-called Don't Ask, Don't Tell (DADT) policy wherein the military does not inquire whether a person is gay, and the person is not required to inform the military if he is gay, has been repealed. Now, a soldier, a sailor, a Marine, or an Air Force pilot can serve openly as a gay man.

For our purposes, it is illuminating to examine the arguments recently put forth about why being gay is incompatible with being a warrior. The rules for the United States military before repeal of DADT state:

> (13) The prohibition against homosexual conduct is a longstanding element of military law that continues to be necessary in the unique circumstances of military service.
>
> (14) The armed forces must maintain personnel policies that exclude persons whose presence in the armed forces would create an unacceptable risk to the armed forces' high standards of morale, good order and discipline, and unit cohesion that are the essence of military capability.
>
> (15) The presence in the armed forces of persons who demonstrate a propensity or intent to engage in homosexual acts would create an unacceptable risk to the high standards of morale, good order, and discipline, and unit cohesion that are the essence of military capability.[1]

This argument against gays in the American military, then, focuses on the potential problem of gay soldiers disrupting "morale, good order and discipline" and especially "unit cohesion." Such contentions asserting that heterosexual men can only bond in combat with other heterosexual men contradicts not only experience, since gay men have been serving with distinction in the armed forces of this and other countries, but also a long historical tradition.

As we have already seen, intense male-male affection, even in the form of genital physical relations, has been a crucial element of the warrior code and the training of the warrior from the time of Homer and into the training of the Spartans and the samurai. Rather than being incompatible with the life of the fighter, male love has been and still is the *sine qua non* of the warrior and the basis of the intense loyalty, even to death, felt toward fellow warriors. In the all-male world of the Trojan and Greek fighters and up to the homosocial universe of the United States Marine Corps, affect is directed to other men although sexual practice is highly regulated. The exemplary warrior, Achilles, was so bound to Patroclus that only the death of his paramour in combat with Hector could rouse Achilles to battle. The strongest emotional relationship in the life of Alexander the Great was with his friend, general, and bodyguard Hephaestion, the son of a Macedonian noble. In the military state of Sparta and in the feudal Japan of the samurai, indoctrination into the warrior culture involved sexual penetration by mentors to solidify allegiance to other warriors. For the Athenians, the homoerotic basis of their society generated the strong bonds, "unit cohesion" writ large, of their powerful and successful army. As Phaedrus states in *The Symposium,* "If there was any mechanism for producing a city or army consisting of lovers and boyfriends, there could be no better form of social organization than this."[2]

"The Manly Love of Comrades" and Democratic Man

If love of man for man defines man as warrior, male bonding has defined democratic man from the very origins of democracy in classical Athens.

In the mid-nineteenth century, the great American poet Walt Whitman chanted his vision of a new democratic nation held together by bonds of comradeship, of fellow feeling that he limned in unmistakably physical homoerotic figures of men embracing:

Come, I will make the continent indissoluble,
I will make the most splendid race the sun ever shone upon,

I will make divine magnetic lands,
> With the love of comrades,
> With the life-long love of comrades.
I will plant companionship thick as trees along all the rivers of
> America, and along the shores of the great lakes, and all
> over the prairies,
I will make inseparable cities, with their arms about each other's necks,
> By the love of comrades,
> By the manly love of comrades.[3]

Whitman's sense that erotic feeling between men is the indissoluble bond of a society based upon equality continues the traditions of the very first democracy, classical Athens. Indeed, it can be argued that democracy arose and was brought to the perfection of participatory democracy in a society where the bonds between men were forged by homoerotic feeling and practice. Public activities were informed by a strong sense of unity with other men grounded in the homoerotic relations between adult citizens and adolescent boys about to become citizens. As Pausanias argues in *The Symposium*, a tyranny such as Persia demands that all love be channeled to the tyrant. A democracy is defined by the love of men for each other. It is worth recalling his words as we consider the Whitmanesque argument for the grounding of America democracy in the "manly love of comrades": "In the Persian Empire the rule is that love-affairs are wrong. In Persia, it is because of their tyrannical government that they condemn them, as well as intellectual and athletic activities. No doubt, it doesn't suit their government that their subjects should have big ideas or develop strong friendships and personal bonds, which are promoted by all these activities, especially by love."[4] Even though women have entered positions of power within the highest reaches of our federal, state, and local governments, our current American democracy is still, if vestigially, based upon male bonding. Governments at all levels retains a bit of the old boys club aura in which friendship between men provides the relationship that drives the making of laws.[5]

Homophobia Past and Present

There is, then, in the West a long tradition of homoerotic bonds as natural and universal, and as essential to the formation of positive masculine identities, especially of the warrior and democratic man. And yet, we can also trace a powerful Western tradition of homophobia, the hatred and fear of men and women who feel same-sex desire and engage in same-sex practices. Strictures against same-sex erotics appear in the Hebrew Bible, continue with intensity into the formation of Christianity, and run with changing justifications and even with increased energy to the present day. The incorporation of homoeroticism into ideals of manliness in the Western world thus runs in parallel with its being proscribed and punished by religious and civil law. Indeed, praise of male love and homophobia seem to engage in a self-reinforcing dynamic in which the increase of one strengthens the other.

To make a rather large generalization, homoerotic desire and practice have been condemned within Judeo-Christian ethics. Same-sex sex is proscribed directly in the Hebrew Bible. Leviticus states, "Thou shalt not lie with mankind, as with womankind: it is an abomination" (18:22), and "If a man also lie with mankind, as he lieth with a woman, both of them have committed an abomination: they shall surely be put to death; their blood shall be upon them" (20:13). Christianity reads the story of the destruction of the city of Sodom by God (Genesis 18–19) as a punishment for the homosexual practices of the city, hence the term "sodomy" in common use for sexual acts between males.

The teachings of the Christian Apostles also condemn male-male sexuality. Paul says of such behavior, "Because of this, God gave them over to shameful lusts. Even their women exchanged natural relations for unnatural ones. In the same way, the men also abandoned natural relations with women and were inflamed with lust for one another. Men committed indecent acts with other men, and received in themselves the due penalty for their perversion" (Romans 1:26–27). And in 1 Corinthians 6:9–11, Paul says, "Do you not know that wrongdoers will not inherit the kingdom of God? Do not be deceived! Fornicators, idolaters, adulterers, *arsenokoitēs*, thieves, the greedy, drunkards, revilers, robbers, none of these will inherit the kingdom of God. And this is what some of you used to be. But you were washed, you were sanctified, you were justified in the name of the Lord Jesus Christ and in the Spirit of our God." The term *arsenokoitēs* has been variously interpreted but can be read as referring to those who engage in homosexual practices.

Homophobia, then, continues to inhabit the theological realm with these verses still being cited by Jews and Christians who base their opposition to homosexuality on the Word of God. Orthodox Jews, as we have seen, regard homoerotic acts as well as gay marriage as grave violations of the Law of God. The practice of male-male sex continues to be categorized as a sin by the Roman Catholic Church, and the Church vigorously opposes gay marriage. Within such theological discourse, gay sex is unnatural in the sense of not following God's plan.

And yet the history of male desire is always complex and often contradictory. The Bible is also quoted by supporters of homosexuality for its touching account of the intense relation between men, experienced by David, one of the most heroic figures of ancient Israel. As a youth, David, the future king of Israel, formed a covenant with King Saul's son, Jonathan, who protected David from Saul's effort to kill him. At the death of Saul and Jonathan in battle, David wrote a lament for both; the portion grieving for Jonathan is now often quoted as praise of gay love:

> I grieve for you,
> My brother Jonathan,
> You were most dear to me.
> Your love was wonderful to me,
> More than the love of women. (2 Samuel 1:26)

With the increasing secularization of the West from the time of the Renaissance, the hostility to same-sex desire and activity shifted from religious discourse based on a reading of the Bible to the nontheological categorization of civil law. Sodomy as sin was replaced by sodomy as crime. Beginning in the sixteenth century, lawmakers in Britain classified homosexual behaviors as criminal in place of priests condemning them as immoral. In the 1530s, during the reign of Henry VIII, England passed the so-called Buggery Act, referring to the term for anal intercourse between men, which made such sexual relations a criminal offense punishable by death. In Britain, "sodomy" remained a capital offense punishable by hanging until 1861. In America, the laws against sodomy varied since they were written by the individual states. After independence, almost all states had laws against male-male anal and oral sex that continued into the twentieth century. Although, as we will see, these laws prohibiting sexual acts even between consenting adults, eventually declared unconstitutional, were upheld by the Supreme Court in the *Bowers v. Hardwick* decision of 1986. This preoccupation with male homosexuality continues in contemporary America where, in spite of the multitude of crucial issues facing America, homosexuality remains central to political debate as seen in the intense conflicts about gay marriage, gays in the military, and warnings about the so-called "gay agenda" taking over the schools.

The criminalization of and occupation with male-male sex in modern times suggest deep social as well as moral pressures to separate same-sex desire and practices from manliness. We can see several reasons for the centrality of homophobia in social discourse. Basically, to return to the opening sentence of this study, manliness can only exist if some men are excluded from the category of men. In the nineteenth century, the emergence of gay culture and the resurgence of homophobia act out a mutually reinforcing dynamic. The strengthening of one strengthens the other. Furthermore, in the modern industrial world, the increasing severity of strictures against male love results from what we have seen as the transformation of male sexuality in the construction of middle-class industrial manhood (see chapter 4). With industrialization, the valorization of the work ethic equated manliness with heterosexual marriage in what can be called the heterosexual marriage imperative. Such channeling of male sexual energy, seen often as spermatic energy, served both to shape man as breadwinner, forced to labor in order to provide for his family; and channeled sex into reproduction so as to avoid sex as pleasure that would draw men's sexual energy away from industrial production. Gay identity in the nineteenth century with its emphasis on aesthetic enjoyment formed itself in self-consciousness opposition to this construction of bourgeois manliness.

This severity of the attack on the perceived threat of the emergent gay culture is epitomized by the Labouchere Amendment, passed in England in 1885 and named after its sponsor in Parliament.[6] This change in the law criminalized male-male sexual behavior defined in the vaguest of terms. The Amendment is notable for not including women and for including the term "gross indecency," which condemns homosexual activity for violating social norms rather than universal ethical laws. The text reads: "Any male person who, in public or private, commits, or is a party to the commission of, or procures, or attempts to procure the commission by any male person of, any act of gross indecency shall be guilty of misdemeanour, and being convicted shall be liable at the discretion of the Court to be imprisoned for any term not exceeding two years, with or without hard labour." It is under this rubric of "gross indecency" that Oscar Wilde was tried in the historically significant trial that for decades defined the identity of the homosexual.

To look ahead—it was not until 1967 that the Sexual Offences Act in Britain decriminalized homosexual acts in private, providing that the act be consensual and both men have reached the age of twenty-one. In 2000, the age of consent in British was reduced to sixteen to conform to the law governing heterosexual sexual acts.

In America, the Bowers decision of 1986 sustaining criminal laws against male same-sex activities between consenting adults was overturned by the

Supreme Court in the case of *Lawrence v. Texas* in 2003. The Court ruling is worth quoting as illustrating the cultural shift in America to acceptance of consenting sex between adult men:

> Houston police entered petitioner Lawrence's apartment and saw him and another adult man, petitioner Garner, engaging in a private, consensual sexual act. Petitioners were arrested and convicted of deviate sexual intercourse in violation of a Texas statute forbidding two persons of the same sex to engage in certain intimate sexual conduct . . . the fact that a State's governing majority has traditionally viewed a particular practice as immoral is not a sufficient reason for upholding a law prohibiting the practice . . . It does involve two adults who, with full and mutual consent, engaged in sexual practices common to a homosexual lifestyle. Petitioners' right to liberty under the Due Process Clause gives them the full right to engage in private conduct without government intervention.[7]

The decriminalization of "sexual practices common to a homosexual lifestyle" in England and America in the mid-twentieth century did, then, restore the legal right to civil manhood for men who practiced male love.

The Invention of the Homosexual as a Masculine Identity

The strengthening of homophobia along with the emergence of a self-conscious gay subculture at the end of the nineteenth century, a dynamic that continues today, was tied to a crucial paradigm shift in thinking about erotic relations between men. This change is often termed "the invention of the homosexual," the shift from seeing same-sex activity as a set of specific acts punishable by law to seeing homoerotic desire as the totalizing, determining basis of a specific type of man and thus of a specific masculine identity.

The foundational account of this historic shift in the definition of manliness is that of the French philosopher Michel Foucault in the first volume of his essential study *The History of Sexuality*:

> As defined by the ancient civil or canonical codes, sodomy was a category of forbidden acts. . . . The nineteenth-century homosexual became a personage, a past, a case history, and a childhood, in addition to being a type of life, a life form and a morphology. . . . Nothing that went in his total composition was unaffected by his sexuality. It was everywhere present in him: at the root of all his actions because it was their insidious and indefinitely active principle; written immodestly on his face and body because it was a secret that always gave itself away. . . . The homosexual was now a species.[8]

Thus a new masculine identity was created. A man who performed sexual acts with other men now became "the homosexual," a distinct species of man in whom, in Foucault's words, "all his actions" are generated by this "insidious and indefinitely active principle" of same-sex object choice. And just as masculine cannot exist as a category without its defining opposite feminine, so too the homosexual could not exist without the invention of its opposite, the heterosexual, a man whose entire identity is also defined by his sexuality, here by his opposite-sex desire. Men now consist of two and only two species: gay and straight.

The invention of the homosexual as a totalizing masculine identity in the late nineteenth century came about in large measure through the medicalization of sexuality. The question of same-sex desire that had once inhabited theological discourse, moved to the social realm, and now occupied the purportedly scientific and medical domain of knowledge. In the late nineteenth century, physicians, who might be called proto-psychiatrists, and biologists invented the field they called "sexology," the ostensibly scientific study of sex. Within this medical model, forms of sexual desire and sexual practice were categorized as either healthy or unhealthy. Within this paradigm, sex between men was defined as unnatural, abnormal, and unhealthy.

Without any understanding that they were working within a culturally specific norm, sexologists such as the young Sigmund Freud asserted that heterosexual genital sex between a man and a woman and aimed toward reproduction was "normal" or, in medical terms, healthy. Yet, Freud's influential scheme of sexual development is filled with contradiction. For Freud, same-sex desire is not innate, even in a minority of men. Rather, sexual object choice is shaped by the development of each person from infant to adult. For Freud, each person is born with what he calls a libido, a sexual instinct analogous to hunger, a drive for bodily pleasure that is at birth undifferentiated as to object choice.[9] The libido goes through a number of stages, fixed at times on the anal and oral, hindered in its development by having to work through the oedipal issues of love for the mother and desire to kill the rival father. Yet, in spite of his belief in the libido as naturally polymorphous—that is, without an innate object choice—Freud asserted that healthy and mature sexuality for men resided in heterosexuality even though such sexuality was not natural in the sense of being innate but must be achieved.

For the sexologists, not only was sex between men seen as abnormal and thus unmanly, but within heterosexual sex any fixations on certain practices, such as oral sex or fetishism, which prevented genital sex aimed at reproduction were categorized as deviations from the normal and natural. Within the new medical-psychiatric vocabulary of sexology, such nongenital acts were termed "perversions" in diverging from the natural. And thus was invented another type of man and a new masculine identity, a subspecies termed "the pervert," the voyeur or pedophile, whose entire self was determined by his abnormal sexual practices.

This medical model with its purported scientific definition of sexual manliness generated, and continues to generate, great differences of opinion. At the end of the nineteenth century, many argued that the homosexual and the pervert required treatment, what we call therapy, to convert such a man to normal sexual manliness. Such was the context for Freud's invention of psychotherapy. In the late nineteenth century, however, and continuing into our time, there was strong objection to the notion that male-male desire is a disease that demands a cure. Then, as now, some felt that men are born with a preponderance of same-sex erotic desire and that such innate feeling cannot and should not be punished. Others argued that being gay is a choice, and that gay men need to be converted to what society defined as sexual normalcy. In any case, it is striking that the idea of homoerotic desire as disease persisted so long into our own time. The inclusion of same-sex desire as a disorder needing treatment was not fully removed from the *Diagnostic and Statistical Manual of Mental Disorders* (DSM), the definitive guide to mental illness for psychiatric professionals, until 1986.

If the homosexual became a species of man in the West in the late nineteenth century and continues to be so now, the historical question arises as to whether the homosexual as a masculine identity existed before the late nineteenth century. Certainly, although the proper practice of male-male sex was central to the positive definition of men in many societies, there is scant evidence of self-conscious identification of men according to sexual object choice. As we have seen, to the question "Was Plato gay?" the answer is that the question is meaningless since the category did not exist. In classical Athens, erotic desire for a beautiful youth was seen as natural, and an elite adult citizen was expected to engage in a homoerotic relation with an adolescent future citizen. But masculinity was not defined by such relations. Sexual acts with boys were only acts: one element in the complex identity of an Athenian citizen.

Eighteenth-century England, however, provides some evidence of a self-conscious gay subculture of men who defined themselves as gay and gathered in what we would now call gay bars, then called "molly houses." In the perpetual synergistic relation between gay self-definition and social homophobia, anti-gay organizations, here Societies for the Reformation of Manners, arose to watch for and to excite public feeling against these "mollies." There were documented raids on these molly houses; mollies were arrested and prosecuted. As chronicled by George Chauncey in *Gay New York*, in late nineteenth and early twentieth-century New York City, in the Bowery district men who dressed in feminine clothing and worked as male prostitutes were called "fairies." Seen as a third sex, as distinct sex between men and women, the fairies created a gay subculture with their own gathering places.[10]

In late nineteenth-century England and in America, the sexologists' idea that same-sex desire was innate and the primary determinate of personality was internalized by many men. In some cases, such ideas lead men to accept their own erotic feelings and yet question their categorization by society as perverts. A striking example of such self-recognition comes from John Addington Symonds, a notable figure in the late-Victorian literary world, who went so far as confess in his memoir of 1889 that since childhood his libido had been directed toward other men: "Among my earliest recollections I must record certain visions, half-dream, half reverie, which were certainly erotic in their nature. . . . I used to fancy myself crouched upon the floor amid a company of naked adult men. . . . The contact of their bodies afforded me a vivid and mysterious pleasure."[11] And yet Symonds denies that such erotic feeling must be linked to abnormality defined as effeminacy: "Morally and intellectually, in character and tastes and habits, I am more masculine than many men I know who adore women."[12]

Furthermore, the social definition of men with homoerotic feeling as a minority of perverts paradoxically strengthened their sense of belonging to a community of men defined by their sexuality. Rejection by middle-class society, then, in large measure created a gay subculture. And, conversely, the members of that subculture validate their identity by setting it as superior to the hegemonic bourgeois culture.[13]

Homoeroticism had existed as an open secret in nineteenth-century English high culture, particularly in the Anglican Church, in the landed aristocracy, and in all-male Oxford and Cambridge where the chief educational texts were classical literature advocating what was termed "Greek love." In his *Studies in the Renaissance*, the Oxford art critic Walter Pater made the covert overt, especially for the knowledgeable reader in the gay subculture, by praising the homoerotic beauty of Greek statues as well as love between men in the Renaissance.[14] Bonded by classical education, as well as life spent in the all-male society of universities and men's clubs, the elite gay subculture of late-Victorian England gathered under the name "Uranians." The self-naming, as always a step in the formation of a masculine identity, derives for this elite steeped in Greek writing from the praise of the goddess Urania or the "Heavenly Aphrodite" in *The Symposium*. For the speaker Phaedrus, man-boy love "derives from the Heavenly goddess, who has nothing of the female in her but only maleness; so this love is directed at boys. . . . Those inspired with this love are drawn towards the male, feeling affection for what is naturally more vigorous and intelligent."[15] These men of the emergent gay subculture, then, evoked their continuity with the admired elite Athenian culture to validate both their homoerotic proclivities and what they saw as their superior sensibility. Furthermore, the Uranians, men who desired their own sex, thought of themselves and were thought of in sexology as a third sex, as a female desirous of handsome men born into a male body.

The specific, and we must remember historically contingent, form of the body and mind of the homosexual was publicly established through the personality and the tragic fate of the most visible figure in this late nineteenth-century gay subculture—Oscar Wilde. The brilliance of his writing and critical thought epitomizes the accomplishments of this subculture. His notoriety and his fall manifest the intensified homophobia of his time and from which the West is now only beginning to recover.

In the last decades of the nineteenth century, Oscar Wilde inhabited the public world as a celebrity, famous for being famous. Wearing velvet clothing, on tour he lectured to admiring Americans on "The House Beautiful." In London he was famous for his brilliant conversation and wit. He married, had two children, but led a sexual double life. Then as now, such doubleness was widespread, especially in the English aristocracy. But Wilde made his own homosexuality overt rather than covert, an open secret. This secret life forms the subtext of his brilliant and enduring works, the witty play *The Importance of Being Earnest,* where men take a different name in the country and the city, as well the Gothic tale *The Picture of Dorian Gray* with its hidden portrait registering Dorian's unnamed but clearly understood sinful actions with other men. In his real life, Wilde had an increasingly open relationship with the younger, handsome, aristocratic Lord Alfred Douglas, known as Bosie. When Bosie's father publicly accused Wilde of being a sodomite, Wilde foolishly brought Bosie's father, the Marquess of Queensberry, to court for libel. In a series of trials in 1895 that focused the attention of England, evidence was presented of Wilde's sexual relations with "rent boys," young male prostitutes. Wilde was prosecuted under the recently passed Labouchere Amendment for "gross indecency" and, refusing to flee to France, given the severe penalty of two years of hard labor in Reading Gaol, described in his well-known poem "The Ballad of Reading Gaol," written after his release. A broken man, Wilde was forced into exile, dying penniless in a drab room in Paris in 1900.[16]

The importance of Wilde's life and especially of his trial in the formation of gay identity cannot be exaggerated. We must remember that there is not a necessary relation between same-sex inclination or activity with personality and body type. The form of same-sex practice is historically contingent, constructed in a variety of ways in a variety of societies. We have only to consider Achilles or Pericles, as well as the variety of gay styles within the many contemporary American gay subcultures. Furthermore, even in Wilde's time there were available a number of scripts for self-identified gay men. Walt Whitman looked to the muscular artisans of his day and the soldiers of the Union as exemplifying his ideal of manly comradeship. In late nineteenth-century England, an out-of-the-closet gay man, Edward Carpenter, looking across the Atlantic to Whitman advocated a life of simple living, of revived craftsmanship, and of political activism in the cause of socialism.

But in the history of gay identity, such variants are often obscured because in his enormous celebrity and notoriety, Wilde established in the public mind the type of the homosexual that persists to this day. Too often, when we speak of the homosexual, we are speaking of what was then termed "The Wildean type." The Wildean type, as set in the nineteenth century, is a physical species—effeminate, corpulent, soft, flabby, and averse to physical activity.[17] In public consciousness the homosexual as the Wildean type is cerebral—brilliant, witty, aloof, and hyper-verbal. Then, as now, gay identity appears inherently linked to aesthetic culture, to preciousness in design and flamboyance in dress.[18] Furthermore, the Wildean identity, in contrast to the Whitmanesque one that celebrates the working man, looks to a connection with aristocratic manliness in its valorization of a life of leisure and sensual enjoyment that seemingly transcends the work ethic and bourgeois compulsory heterosexuality.

The Wilde trials were a festival of homophobia. The severity of the punishment that destroyed Wilde, the man, set an example that drove homosexuality in England and in America back into the closet, back into the subculture of the secret life until the later twentieth century. It was not until 2003 that "buggery" defined as a crime in the sixteenth century and the offense of "gross indecency" added to the law in the Laborchere Amendment of 1885, and under which Wilde was prosecuted, were removed from English law.

Gay Masculine Identity: Some Issues

Throughout the United States, gay athletic leagues flourish—supervised by the North American Gay Amateur Athletic Alliance. Gay softball, for example, has several hundred teams around the country. These provide comradeship, a sense of community, and a modern riposte to the Wildean stereotype of the homosexual as sedentary and soft. But a problem has arisen. Several members of the softball league have sued for damages because of their expulsion from the Gay Softball World Series for being "nongay." Subject to intense secret interrogation from league officials, one player was found to be married, another admitted to sexual contact with women, others confessed to being bisexual.[19] Whatever the decision as to who will be allowed to play, the lawsuit challenges the assumption on which the gay softball league and gay identity itself are founded—the sharp dualist differentiation between gay and nongay that in this case has to be adjudicated by law.

This severe dichotomy created in the late nineteenth century still works its power on society and on male life. Gay identity is founded on a distinction stamped on our common vocabulary—"Is he gay or straight?" This distinction in defining masculine identity operates with an implacable duality. The powerful word "or" indicates that a man can only be one or the other, a homosexual or a heterosexual.

Rather than adopting the gay/straight dualism, it would be more accurate to think of male sexuality as a continuum with exclusively same-sex and exclusively opposite-sex desire set at the poles and a range or mix of libidinal feelings and sexual practices between these extremes. Such a model allows us to appreciate the blend of libidinal feelings in each man, rather than having to set masculine sexual identity into two, and only two, categories. Indeed, the work of Alfred Kinsey, the noted twentieth-century sex researcher, supplies some experimental proof subverting the dualist scheme by offering evidence of the range and variety of male sexual consciousness and behavior. In his extensive survey of male sexual desire and practice set down in *Sexual Behavior in the Human Male* (1948), Kinsey and his many interviewers work within a seven-point scale of male sexual behavior. At the heterosexual end of this scale or continuum are those men who had "no physical contacts" and "no psychic responses to individuals of their own sex."[20] Toward the middle of the scale are men with "more than incidental homosexual experience . . . but [whose] heterosexual experiences and/or reactions still surpass their homosexual experiences and reactions."[21] At the midpoint on the "heterosexual-homosexual scale" are those who are "about equally homosexual and heterosexual in their overt experience and/or their psychic responses" and who "equally enjoy both types of contacts."[22] For men at the midpoint, Kinsey strikingly does not employ the term "bisexual," which implies the gay/straight dualism. Symmetrically, toward the homosexual end of the scale are individuals ranging from "more overt activity and/or psychic reactions" to "almost entirely" to "exclusively homosexual both in regard to their overt experience and in regard to their psychic reactions."[23] Kinsey's powerful rejection of the heterosexual/homosexual dualism was vilified on publication because the study documented that some degree of homoerotic desire and some participation in homosexual activity can be found in the majority of American men. Kinsey's conclusion is worth quoting at length:

> The histories which have been available in the present study make it apparent that the heterosexuality or homosexuality of many individuals is not an all-or-nothing proposition. . . . There are some whose heterosexual experiences predominate, there are some whose homosexual experiences predominate, there are some who have had equal amounts of both types of experience. . . . Males do not represent two discrete populations, heterosexual and homosexual. The world is not to be divided into sheep and goats. . . . Only the human mind invents categories and tries to force facts into separated pigeon-holes. The living world is a continuum in each and every one of its aspects. The sooner we learn this concerning human sexual behavior the sooner we shall reach a sound understanding of the realities of sex.[24]

So what do the theories of Freud and the surveys of Kinsey tell us of the realities of sex for men and of the gay identity that has become so powerful a script for men in contemporary Europe and America? Certainly, there is reason to believe that to some degree, same-sex orientation is genetic since homoerotic desire is often felt at a very young age, as in the case of Symonds. Certainly, the innate hypothesis implies that social discrimination against gay men is as indefensible as discrimination against men born with nonwhite skin.

As we have seen in our discussion of the nature/nurture issue throughout the history of manliness, the particular form or forms of masculinity available to a man at any historical moment can best be seen as resulting from an interplay of the innate and the socially constructed. So if same-sex orientation is innate in some or in all men, still the importance and the restrictions on such desire vary in specific societies, as our brief historical account of the ancient warrior and classical Athens demonstrates. With the invention of the homosexual as a species in the contemporary world, gay identity for men becomes one possible form of self-identification for a man of homoerotic inclination. Even though under attack by homophobic elements of society, identity as a homosexual is validated by other men who share homoerotic feelings and increasingly accepted by society at large, as seen by the very recent open acceptance of gays in the military.

But it must be emphasized that while a gay identity is now possible for contemporary men, in our world adopting this identity is a matter of choice. In a world offering many choices, to participate in the gay subculture, to inhabit the masculine identity of the homosexual becomes one of many possible ways of defining the self, of having an identity as a man. Gay identity, then, becomes a form of self-identification, of self-fashioning for not all men who feel homoerotic desire or engage in same-sex activity choose to take on a gay male identity. It is one decision to engage in homosexual sex; it is another decision to consider oneself a homosexual, and yet another choice to declare openly that one *is* a homosexual. Gay identity, then, depends not on the innateness or formation of homoerotic desire, but from the decision to define the self both publicly and privately as gay.

Gay history illustrates the centrality of self-identification. If we return to the turn of the nineteenth-century New York chronicled by Chauncey in *Gay New York,* we see that in lower Manhattan, centering on the Bowery and Greenwich Village, men called "fairies" would dress in female clothing and walk the streets. The fairies who solicited sex with men identified themselves as a third sex and were characterized by their effeminacy. Their clients, or johns, were immigrant working-class Irish and Italian men who would pay these males for sex. But these johns did not identify themselves as homosexual or gay simply because they engaged in male-male sex. Indeed, their self-definition depended not on sexual object choice, but on the contrast between their performance of conventional manliness and the womanish unmanly appearance of the fairies. Chauncey perceptively demonstrates how the criteria of manliness can be distinct from sexual practice:

> The abnormality (or "queerness") of the fairy was defined as much by his woman-like character or "effeminacy" as his solicitation of male sexual

partners; the "man" who responded to his solicitations—no matter how often—was not considered abnormal, a homosexual, so long as he abided by masculine gender conventions. Indeed, the centrality of effeminacy to the representation of the "fairy" allowed many conventionally masculine men, especially unmarried men living in sex-segregated immigrant communities, to engage in extensive sexual activity with other men without risking stigmatization and the loss of their status as normal men.[25]

Or consider men in modern life who engage in same-sex sex but who do not identify themselves as homosexuals. Many men in the Kinsey interviews describe homoerotic desire and activity that rank well toward the homosexual end of the scale but do not necessarily define themselves as homosexual. In criticizing theories of innateness, Freud notes "contingent" male-male sex where women are unavailable, and men derive "satisfaction from sexual intercourse" with men.[26] One immediately thinks of men in prison where male-male sex is the norm, where tough men compete for sexual favors from other men who take on the female sexual role of being penetrated much like the fairies of nineteenth-century New York. Similarly, in the African-American community, male-male sex is practiced, even though anti-gay rhetoric is strong. In the British public (that is private) schools for the elite, sex among boys is the norm, but as the boys become adults they marry. As in classical Athens where man-boy sex is normative, the sexual bonds formed in early life do much to hold together the ruling elite.

Gay identity, then, like the other masculine identities discussed, is an amalgam of innate and constructed qualities, in part a social formation rather than wholly an expression of innate characteristics. In our society, unlike say Athens, rather than setting a single script for men the culture offers many possible ways of being a man. A masculine identity is not thrust upon a man at birth but can be chosen. So the simple term "gay" might best be replaced by the increasingly popular locution of "gay identified" to foreground gay identity as a choice of how to present the self to the world and which among many subcultures a man may decide to inhabit.

To return to the gay softball league's problem of distinguishing the gay from the nongay—the officials acknowledge that they see the problem of "how to define 'gay.' How do you prove if someone is gay or straight?" Acknowledging the problems of a narrow definition that does not fit the full range of male sexual behavior, the organization finally adopted the simple criterion of self-identification: "The North American Gay Amateur Athletic

Alliance has changed its definition of gay to include bisexual and transgender people. It also clarified that it would determine sexual orientation by self-declaration."[27]

The problem of determining who is gay extends beyond membership in a baseball league. Within a pervasive cultural homophobia, the homosexual/heterosexual dualism also generates a problem for those men who choose to inhabit a heterosexual identity. Many men feel a deep interior unease about sexual identity. The question of "Am I really gay?" is internalized. Such anxiety is strengthened by the intermixture in all men of same-sex and opposite-sex desire and intensified by the social cost for most men of being classified in the public sphere as being gay. Taken to an extreme, this personal fear of "being a homosexual" can morph into what is termed "homosexual panic" often manifested in an extreme homophobia functioning to mask one's own homoerotic impulses.

Furthermore, given a homophobia grounded in a severe dualism, male power inevitably generates male anxiety. Within a patriarchal society, close bonds between men are the foundations of power. And men do form affective homosocial relationships. But with the invention of the homosexual as the type of the unmanly, any close relations between men can come perilously close to the forbidden behavior of the homosexual. And since to be labeled a homosexual is to be excluded from manliness and thus from power; and given the centrality of male bonding as the foundation of male power, all men live within a state of anxiety that is another form of homosexual panic. The foundational statement of this inherent connection between patriarchy, male sexual angst, and homophobia is set out in the influential work of Eve Kosofsky Sedgwick: "Because the paths of male entitlement, especially in the nineteenth century, required certain intense male bonds that were not readily distinguishable from the most reprobated bonds, an endemic and eradicable state of what I am calling male homosexual panic became the normal condition of male heterosexual entitlement."[28] A quick thought experiment will demonstrate that the more intense the bonds in any traditionally all-male organization, such as a fire department, the police, or the Marine Corps, the more intense the homophobia—the more intense the fear of being considered a faggot by one's comrades. In a culture where homoerotic desire is abhorred, the psychological defense mechanism of homophobia is strongest where the intimacy of male-male bonds is deepest.

Paradoxically, then, the formation of homosexual identity has been a source of liberation for some men, but for men who are not gay-identified has generated inhibition in the affectionate relations between men that characterized earlier cultures. The very existence of a gay identity within a homophobic world has made many identified as heterosexual fearful of showing affection or physical fondness for other men since an action like touching the skin of another man, to take one example, may cross the line between the acceptable and the forbidden and thus lead to the social consequences of being labeled gay. In the homosocial continuum—that is, the continuity between homosocial and homosexual relations between men— the boundary line in behavior that differentiates the straight from the gay, the homosocial from the homoerotic has been constantly shifting. Can men now write warm letters to other men without fear of being considered gay, as they did in the nineteenth-century age of "passionate friendship"? If athletes can pat each others' rumps on the playing field, can men do the same in a barroom? Can men hold hands as they do in Arab lands? Can men kiss?

Conclusion

Masculine Identities Now

In our time, traditional manliness is besieged. Some lament that the long-established attributes of masculinity—physical strength, aggressiveness, the power of individual effort, heterosexual virility, and the domination of women—no longer seem functional for men in the modern world of computer programming, corporate hierarchies, gay liberation, and gender equality. But for others, to lament the passing of historical ideals of manliness may be in itself a masculinist activity. The liberatory movements of the twentieth and twenty-first centuries—for women, for blacks, and for gay men—can be seen as opening new possibilities that can enrich the lives of men. Yet whatever one's views about the so-called crisis of masculinity, there seems to be no question but that many elements of contemporary life have destabilized masculine identity.[1]

A man's sense of himself depends upon his work, but the triumph of capitalism in Europe and America has made precarious the masculine role of breadwinner. Corporations now easily and quickly move manufacturing from place to place within the United States and from the United States to low-wage countries. The traditional social contract between employer and employee based on mutual responsibility and that had assured employment, employee benefits, and employee loyalty has disappeared as owners shift to less expensive hiring on short-term contracts. Employment has returned to the cash-nexus of the first days of the industrial revolution (see chapter 4). As I write, with the replacement of men by machines and the movement of manufacturing from America overseas, joblessness in the United States has soared. Predictions are that high unemployment and insecure employment will be the new normal. The long lines of desperate men seeking work show men who have lost their primary identity as men.

If globalization and computerization have weakened the self-definition of man as worker, so, too, the success of feminism attaining to a great degree equal opportunity for women has challenged ideas of manliness, not merely in the competition with men for jobs, but in the basic definition of masculinity. As we have noted many times, the definition of the masculine can only exist in its difference from its presumed opposite, the feminine. Men are men in that they are not women. But if females no longer act in conventionally feminine ways and instead act in conventionally masculine ones, then the difference that grounds masculine identity simply disappears.

To put the matter differently, in tracking the history of manliness, we have not questioned the most basic assumption about manliness—that certain qualities defined as manly are linked to the male body. We have considered manliness only as the behavior of those born biological males. But, as Judith Halberstam, the influential advocate of female masculinity writes, "Masculinity must not and cannot and should not reduce down to the male body and its effects."[2] If we consider masculinities as primarily social constructions rather than as expressions of biological qualities of males, then the scripts of manliness can just as easily be performed by biological females: "What we understand as heroic masculinity has been produced by and across both male and female bodies."[3] Indeed, Halberstam notes a number of examples of what she terms female masculinity, that is, traditionally masculine traits acted out by female-born persons. She cites the figure of the tomboy, as well as female Olympic athletes and film roles celebrating powerful muscular females battling aliens or robots of the future. Yet she also notes that as in the case of tomboys who are pressured to adopt conventionally female qualities as they reach puberty, female masculinity has been opposed by patriarchal society anxious to maintain the privileges of male-born persons by being able "to wed masculinity to maleness and to power and domination."[4] Thus, if we accept the reality of female masculinity, we must revise our terminology for manliness to employ the category of male masculinity to describe qualities defined as manly being performed by male-born persons.

Furthermore, the link of masculinity to the male body is further challenged by the recognition that being born biologically a male does not necessarily generate an internal sense that one really is a male. Some men deeply feel inside that they are not men. Increasingly and with increased public acceptability, persons born as biological men see themselves as transgender persons, that is, people whose gender identity differs from that usually associated with their birth sex—as in the case of males who feel that are women born in a man's body. We could rephrase the statement with which we began this history—"that all men are not men"—to include the qualification "all men do not believe they are men."

And with new technologies in surgery and hormone therapy, transgender feelings can be translated into reshaping the physical body. The dissolution of masculinity can be applied to the male body itself. A biological male can be changed into a biological female, into a female body, or into a body that is a mix of male and female physiology. The existence of transsexuals, persons who have been transformed from one biological sex to another, then destabilizes the ancient notion of the stability of the male body as unchangeably male and also subverts the power of the two-sex model, the basis of manliness, that assumes one is born either a male or a female. As we now must speak not only in the new categories of male masculinity and female masculinity, to be accurate, we must describe the biology of sex not in terms of *men* and *women* but of *male-born* persons and *female-born* persons.

As the most basic assumptions that underlie masculinity have been challenged, so have the traditional cultural scripts of male performance that we term manliness—primarily because of changing economic conditions and the increasing equality of women. Within the Western definition, manliness was marked by a predatory and rapacious virility as men could, as in the *Iliad,* exchange women between them. In modern times, men could gain sex from women not only through force but primarily through their wealth and patriarchal power. Women were in no position to refuse men because sexual favors provided one of the only means of gaining financial security, as through marriage in bourgeois society. The way to money depended on the attraction of the sexual female body and the promise of submission.

But as women have gained economic power, for men, wealth and social status no longer suffice as a way to get girls. Traditional masculine qualities no longer succeed in what Darwin called sexual selection: developing qualities the male of the species needs to attract females. In this society of gender equality, men have adapted by adopting what has been called the female position, the traditional female strategy in sexual selection that employs the attraction of the body and social charm. Consider the celebrated rise of the sensitive man, the man who is empathetic, who listens, who even cries. The extreme case of the erotic attraction of the male body for women may be the Chippendale dancers, physically attractive men in tight skimpy costumes who perform sexual dances for female delectation. In the popular movie *The Full Monty,* having lost their jobs in a decaying English industrial town and thus deprived of their breadwinner role, a group of unemployed men, in order to make money and thus reassert their manhood, entertain women in a parody of female burlesque, finally showing off their physical manhood by going the "full monty." Men going to the gym to work on their abs, a new masculine obsession, in part stems from a nostalgic desire to restore to masculine identity the physicality no longer developed through manual labor, and also from the need to become physically attractive to women since patriarchal power and wealth no longer succeed.

Indeed, contemporary men have adopted other traditionally feminine qualities due in part to changing economics in which women take on the formerly specifically masculine identity of breadwinner. Many men now take on the role of nurturing mother in the domestic sphere, a position historically assigned to women. Men now share child-rearing duties with their wives, and some men have become full-time fathers. The single dad and stay-at-home dad are entirely new identities for male life. And this child-raising by men departs from the separate spheres of the past where the mother supplies the unconditional love, the father the harsh discipline asserted with cane or belt. Gone are the days of the mother saying, "Wait till your father comes home." The man now nurtures. Fathers can, and are expected to, express warmth and unconditional love for their children.

As men increasingly adopt the female position in their lives, the sharp boundary between heterosexual/homosexual, gay/straight invented by sexologists in the late nineteenth century appears to be dissolving. Many heterosexually oriented men now adopt the lifestyle conventionally associated not only with women, but also with many men within the gay subculture by manifesting an interest in fashion, and clothing. The term metrosexual nicely encapsulates this identity of a metropolitan, that is, an urban sophisticated man showing an interest in personal elegance, who is still self-identified as a heterosexual.

Indeed, as straight metrosexual men perform in the mode conventionally associated with gay men, so men can increasingly, without shame or danger, feel and perform same-sex affection without sex. Intense nonsexual bonding between men has been central to America culture as in the trip downriver of Huck and Jim in the classic *Adventures of Huckleberry Finn* and in modern times in the ubiquitous buddy films such as *Butch Cassidy and the Sundance Kid* (1969). Increasingly, American films have made what the nineteenth century called passionate friendship more central and more open as in such films as *I Love you Man* (2009) and *Old Joy* (2006). There is even a newly minted term for the ancient tradition of affection between men. "Bromance," nicely fusing *brother* and *romance*, describes a love between males on the model of deep affection between brothers. This new word for male-male affection nicely restores to our language the unashamed recognition of the enriching power of strong caring between men denoted in the Greek term *philia,* describing the bond between warriors (see chapter 1). The acceptance of bromance in film and in the life of men challenges the pervasive male anxiety that any sign of fondness for another man would lead to public shaming as a homosexual.

Of course, every reaction has a counterreaction. That some men now show the emotional sensitivity and nurturing traditionally associated with the female and perform the fashion sense linked to certain gay styles, other men have, with intensity and in defense of their manliness, reasserted traditional masculinity. The rise of a macho, aggressive style and dominating male-centered sexuality informs contemporary life in parallel with the domestication and even emasculation of American men. Presidential campaigns are fought over the question of which candidate is more virile. Warriors such as Navy Seals are the new American heroes. If some films show sensitive men drawn to each other, other films draw their audience with hypermasculine heroes such as Sylvester Stallone, George Segal, and Bruce Willis. The cult movie *Fight Club* offers a satisfying male fantasy of a secret society where overtly respectable young professionals meet clandestinely to box with each other in an assertion of what is represented as an authentic but socially repressed male identity. Professional American football with its bruising body contact of overly large men has become America's favorite sport. The self-made man of business is the new celebrity. And with this hero worship of the traditional identities of the warrior and the businessman, there has been a backlash against new and challenging forms of masculinity, as in the attack on the intellectual man derided as the nerd or geek.

In contrast to the warrior societies that fought at Troy or the democracy of Athens, contemporary society does not exhibit a unitary form of manliness nor even a hegemonic masculinity. The scripts of manliness and the possibilities for male lives have multiplied and shifted with an increasing acceleration. Recent liberation movements—black, women's, and gay—have surely challenged traditional masculinity and the self-esteem of those men who inhabit such conventional identities. Yet these movements have also opened the possibility of liberation in the lives of men. Although there are external and internalized pressures to conform to the traditions of manliness, there is a potential, perhaps not yet fully realized, to invent new forms of manliness. As we have seen, in the modern world masculine identities are no longer necessarily determined by birth but rather can be formed through conscious choice among possibilities. Our new vocabulary accurately registers the vast and liberatory change. No longer do we say a man *is* black or gay or Jewish, but that he is black-identified, gay-identified, or Jewish-identified. Masculine identity now implies self-identification. The options have widened. Masculine identity is now, to a great degree, a matter of choice.

Notes

Introduction

1. See David D. Gilmore, *Manhood in the Making: Cultural Concepts of Masculinity* (New Haven, CT: Yale University Press, 1990).

2. For the definitive history of the one-sex and the two-sex models, see Thomas Laquer, *Making Sex: Body and Gender from the Greeks to Freud* (Cambridge, MA: Harvard University Press, 1992).

3. "South African Is Cleared to Compete as a Woman," *New York Times,* July 7, 2010, B13.

4. Anne Fausto-Sterling, "The Sexe Which Prevaileth," in *The Masculinity Studies Reader,* eds. Rachel Adams and David Savran (Malden, MA: Blackwell, 2002), 383.

5. Anne Fausto-Sterling, "How to Build a Man," in *Sexuality,* ed., Robert Nye (Oxford: Oxford University Press, 1999), 236.

6. Don Kulick, "The Gender of Brazilian Transgendered Prostitutes," in Adams, ed., *Masculinity Studies Reader,* 390.

7. Michel Foucault, *Herculine Barbin (Being the Recently Discovered Memoirs of a Nineteenth Century French Hermaphrodite)* (New York: Vintage, 1980).

8. Judith Butler, *Gender Trouble* (New York: Routledge, 1999), xv.

Chapter 1 Man as Warrior

1. Homer, *The Iliad.* Trans. Robert Fagles (New York: Penguin, 1990). All citations to *The Iliad* are from this superb translation.

2. Plato, *The Symposium* (New York: Penguin, 1999), 219e–221d.

3. Maxine Hong Kingston, *The Woman Warrior: Memoirs of a Girlhood among Ghosts* (New York: Vintage, 1989).

4. William Scott Wilson, *Ideals of the Samurai: Writings of Japanese Warriors* (New York: Black Belt Communications, 1982), 62.

5. Daisetz Teitaro Suzuki, *Zen and Japanese Culture* (Princeton, NJ: Princeton University Press, 1938), 78.

6. Ibid.

7. Ibid.

8. Yukio Mishima, *Patriotism* (New York: New Directions, 2010).

9. Plutarch, *On Sparta* (London: Penguin, 2005), 18–19.

10. Ernst Junger, *Storm of Steel.* 1920. (New York: Penguin, 2004), 255.

11. See the fine discussion of the language of personal relations in Jonathan Shay, *Achilles in Vietnam: Combat Trauma and the Undoing of Character* (New York: Simon & Schuster, 1994), 40–43.

12. Quoted in Shay, *Achilles,* 40.

13. Steven E. Ambrose, *Band of Brothers: E Company, 506th Regiment, 101st Airborne from Normandy to Hitler's Eagle's Nest* (New York: Simon & Schuster, 2001).

14. Shakespeare, *Henry V,* act 5, scene 3.

15. Official website, U.S. Marine Corps, www.marines.com.

16. Homer, *The Iliad,* book 2, 366–70.

17. Viking Answer Lady, www.vikinganswerlady.com/berserke.shtml.

18. Junger, *Storm of Steel,* 232.

19. Quoted in Shay, *Achilles,* 83.

20. Quoted in Shay, *Achilles,* 83.

21. See the fine discussion of PTSD throughout Shay, *Achilles.*

22. Ralph Waldo Emerson, "Hymn: Sung at the Completion of the Concord Monument," in *American Poetry: The Nineteenth Century,* vol. 1, ed. John Hollander (New York: New American Library, 1993), 318–19, II: 1–4.

23. Chernow, *George Washington* (New York: Penguin, 2010. Kindle edition), location 3985.

24. Tim O'Brien, "The Things They Carried," in *The Norton Anthology of Short Fiction: Shorter Seventh Edition,* ed. Richard Bausch (New York: Norton, 2006), 613.

25. Official website, U.S. Marine Corps, www.marines.com.

26. Ibid.

27. Soldier's Creed, Army Values, www.army.mil/values/soldiers.html.

28. Thayer Evans, "Bruised and Beaten, Favre Is Again Unsure of Future," *New York Times* (January 25, 2010), D6.

Chapter 2 Athens and the Emergence of Democratic Man

1. Werner Jaeger, *Paideia: the Ideals of Greek Culture* (New York: Oxford University Press, 1945), 239.

2. Pericles, "Funeral Oration," 3, www.fordham.edu/halsall/ancient/pericles-funeralspeech.html.

3. Ibid.

4. Ibid.

5. Ibid.

6. The definitive account of this Athenian ideal and of its historical influence can be found in Jaeger, *Paideia.*

7. See chapter 3 for discussion of the training of classical craftsmen.

8. For an image of this celebrated statue and its history, see http://www.britishmuseum.org/explore/highlights/highlight_objects/gr/d/discus-thrower_discobolus.aspx.

9. Kenneth Clark, *The Nude: A Study in Ideal Form* (New York: Anchor, 1956), 239–42.

10. Joseph Roisman, *The Rhetoric of Manhood: Masculinity in the Attic Orators* (Berkeley: University of California Press, 2005), 105–29. The discussion of Athenian martial values is throughout indebted to this volume.

11. Pericles, "Funeral Oration."

12. Ibid.

13. Roisman, *Rhetoric of Manhood*, 129.

14. Plato, *Symposium*. 220e, 221a.

15. Ibid., 184d.

16. Ibid. 179a.

17. George Orwell, *1984* (New York: Signet, 1949).

18. Plato, *Symposium*, 182d.

19. Ibid., 210a–12a.

20. Ibid., 212d.

21. Ibid., 214a

22. Ibid., 219c, d.

23. Quoted in Donald Kagan, *Pericles of Athens and the Birth of Democracy* (New York: Free Press, 1991), 37. This account of Pericles is indebted to Kagan's fine study of Pericles as exemplifying the Athenian ideal of manhood.

24. Quoted in Kagan, *Pericles,* 86.

25. Kagan, *Pericles,* 3.

26. For a full account and images of the Parthenon frieze, see Greek Ministry of Culture, www.ekt.gr.

27. Pericles, "Funeral Oration."

28. For a superb account of the relation of Lincoln's Gettysburg Address to Pericles's Funeral Oration and to Athenian manhood in general, see Gary Wills, *Lincoln at Gettysburg: The Words that Remade America* (New York: Simon & Schuster, 1992).

Chapter 3 The Craftsman

1. Richard Sennett, *The Craftsman* (New York: Penguin, 2009), 9.

2. Alison Burford, *Craftsmen in Greek and Roman Society* (Ithaca, NY: Cornell University Press, 1972), 14. The account of craftsmen in the classical world is indebted to this excellent book.

3. See the discussion of Cellini and his salt cellar in Sennett, *The Craftsman,* 67–75.

4. Homer, "Hymn to Hephaestus."

5. Burford, *Craftsmen*, 14.

6. Ibid., 159–60.

7. Mary Beard, *Pompeii* (London: Profile Books, 2008). 294–95 and Plate 5.

8. Burford, *Craftsmen*, 212–13.

9. Ibid., 212.

10. For an image of this celebrated statue and its history, see http://www.britishmuseum.org/explore/highlights/highlight_objects/gr/d/discus-thrower_discobolus.aspx.

11. Quoted in Burford, *Craftsmen*, 12.

12. See Sennett, *The Craftsman*, for a fine general defense of craft as expanding the mind as well as the senses.

13. Beard, *Pompeii*, 59 and Plate 21.

14. See account in Burford, *Craftsmen*, 71–72.

15. Ibid., 102.

16. For a general account of the rise of the machine and its threat to handicraft, see Herbert Sussman, *Victorian Technology: Invention, Innovation, and the Rise of the Machine* (Santa Barbara, CA: Praeger, 2009), Chapter 1.

17. Richard Russo, "High and Dry," *Granta* no. 111 (Summer 2010), 205.

18. Ibid., 206.

19. For a description and images of this structure, see www.victorianstation.com/palace.html.

20. John Ruskin, "The Nature of Gothic," [1851–53], *The Norton Anthology of English Literature* (New York: Norton, 2000), 2:1436.

21. Henry Wadsworth Longfellow, "The Village Blacksmith," in *American Poetry: The Nineteenth Century,* vol. I, 375–77.

22. New York Plumbers Local Union 1, www:ualocal1.org.

23. Ibid.

Chapter 4 Economic Man and the Rise of the Middle Class

1. For a history of mechanization and its social consequences in England, see Sussman, *Victorian Technology.*

2. For an image of this celebrated statue, see http://www.britishmuseum.org/explore/highlights/highlight_objects/gr/d/discus-thrower_discobolus.aspx.

3. Thomas Carlyle, *Past and Present.* 1843. (Boston: Houghton Mifflin, 1965), 196.

4. This painting can be seen at www.victorianweb.org/painting/fmb/paintings/2.html.

5. Ford Madox Ford, *Ford Madox Brown: A Record of His Life and Work* (London: Longmans, 1896), 190. See also the discussion of this painting in regard to

the formation of masculinity in industrial society in Herbert Sussman, *Victorian Masculinities: Manhood and Masculine Poetics in Early Victorian Literature and Art* (Cambridge: Cambridge University Press, 1995), 39–41.

6. Carlyle, *Past and Present,* 179.

7. Ralph Waldo Emerson, "Self-Reliance," [1841], www.gutenberg.org/files/16643/16643-h/16643-h.htm.

8. Samuel Smiles, *Self-Help: with illustrations of Conduct and Perseverance.* 1859. (London: IEA Health and Welfare Unit, 1996), 1–2.

9. Ibid.

10. www.quotationspage.com

11. Charles Dickens, *A Christmas Carol.* 1843. (New York: Bantam, 1986).

12. Charles Dickens, *Great Expectations.* 1861. (London: Penguin, 2002).

13. F. Scott Fitzgerald, *The Great Gatsby.* 1925, in *Three Novels of F. Scott Fitzgerald* (New York: Scribner's, 1953).

14. Ibid., 91.

15. Ibid., 137.

16. For an account of the rise of all-male societies in the nineteenth century as anti-marriage institutions, see Sussman, *Victorian Masculinities,* 4–5.

17. See Sussman, *Victorian Technology,* 51–53.

18. Nye, *Sexuality,* 137.

19. For the definitive account of the reconceptualization of the male body as an engine, see Anson Rabinbach, *The Human Motor: Energy, Fatigue, and the Origins of Modernity* (Berkeley: University of California Press, 1992).

Chapter 5 I Am a Man: African-American Masculine Identities

1. For images, see Memphis Sanitation Workers' Strike at www.digitaljournalist.org. The words "I AM A MAN" echo the emblem of the British abolitionist movement of the late eighteenth century showing a black man in chains saying "Am I Not a Man and a Brother?" See the image at "Am I Not a Man . . . " at www.websters-dictionary-online.com.

2. Frederick Douglass, *Narrative of the Life of Frederick Douglass, an American Slave.* 1845. (New York: Barnes & Noble, 2003), 17.

3. Ibid.

4. Ibid., 49.

5. Ibid., 69.

6. For an analysis of the trickster in African-American literature, see Henry Louis Gates, Jr., *The Signifying Monkey: A Theory of African-American Literary Criticism* (New York: Oxford University Press, 1989).

7. Douglass, *Narrative,* 67.

8. Ibid., 26.

9. Ibid.

10. Ibid., 41.

11. Ibid., 96.

12. Malcolm X, *The Autobiography of Malcolm X.* 1964. (New York: Ballantine, 1973). Another powerful modern autobiography indebted to the slave narrative is Richard Wright, *Black Boy.* 1954. (New York: Library of America, 1991).

13. Malcolm X, *Autobiography,* 31.

14. Ibid., 166.

15. Ibid., 203.

16. For the definitive treatment of Lincoln and slavery, see Eric Foner, *The Fiery Trial: Abraham Lincoln and American Slavery* (New York: Norton, 2010).

17. Quoted in Foner, *Fiery Trial,* 256.

18. Ibid., 286.

19. Douglass, *Narrative,* 67–68.

20. See an account of Lincoln's belief in colonization in Foner, *Fiery Trial,* 215–59.

21. Frantz Fanon, *Black Skin, White Masks,* in Adams, Rachel and David Savran, eds. *The Masculinity Studies Reader* (Malden: Blackwell, 2002), 241.

22. Ibid., 240.

23. Darryl Pinckney, "The Two Conversions of Malcolm X," *The New York Review of Books* 58 (September 29, 2011), 72.

24. Barack Obama, *Dreams from My Father: A Story of Race and Inheritance* [1995] (New York: Crown, 2007), 86.

25. Orlando Paterson, "Race Unbound" (*New York Times Book Review* September 25, 2011), 12. Review of Touré, *Who's Afraid of Post-Blackness* (New York: Free Press, 2011).

26. Ibid.

27. Ibid.

Chapter 6 Jewish-American Masculine Identities

1. For a provocative account of how the definition of manliness within Rabbinic Judaism might provide a model for a viable contemporary masculinity, see Daniel Boyarin, *Unheroic Conduct: The Rise of Heterosexuality and the Invention of the Jewish Man* (Berkeley: University of California Press, 1997).

2. The text of Washington's letter can be found at www.tourosynagogue.org/pdfs/WashingtonLetter.pdf.

3. Isaac Babel, "Odessa Stories," in *Isaac Babel: Collected Stories* (New York: Penguin, 1994), 237–321.

4. For a readable and admiring account of American Jewish gangsters, see Rich Cohen, *Tough Jews: Fathers, Sons, and Gangster Dreams* (New York: Vintage, 1999).

5. See especially such stories as "Eli, the Fanatic" and "The Conversion of the Jews," in Philip Roth, *Goodbye Columbus and Five Short Stories.* 1959. (New York: Vintage, 1994).

Chapter 7 Same-Sex Desire and Masculine Identity

1. U.S. Code: Policy concerning homosexuality in the armed forces. Title 10 > Subtitle a > Part ii > Chapter 37 > § 654.

2. Plato, *Symposium,* 178e.

3. Walt Whitman, "For You O Democracy," *Leaves of Grass,* ed. Sculley Bradley and Harold Blodgett (New York: Norton, 1973), 117.

4. Plato, *Symposium,* 182d.

5. Eve Kosofsky Sedgwick, in her foundational examination of the ties between men, uses the example of the bonds between President Ronald Reagan and Jesse Helms, a conservative senator, to illustrate the shifting boundary line between the homosocial and the homoerotic. *Between Men: English Literature and Male Homosocial Desire* (New York: Columbia University Press, 1985), 3.

6. For a fine account of homophobia, the closet, and literature in late nineteenth-century England, see Elaine Showalter, *Sexual Anarchy: Gender and Culture at the Fin de Siècle* (New York: Viking, 1990).

7. Lawrence v. Texas (02–102), 539 U.S. 558 (2003), 41 S.W. 3d 349, http://www.law.cornell.edu/supct/html/02–102.ZS.html.

8. Michel Foucault, *The History of Sexuality: Volume I: An Introduction* (New York: Vintage, 1990), 43.

9. Sigmund Freud, *Three Essays on the Theory of Sexuality,* trans. and ed. James Strachey (New York: Basic Books, 1962). In Nye, *Sexuality,* 186.

10. George Chauncey, *Gay New York: Gender, Urban Culture, and the Making of the Gay Male World 1890–1940* (New York: Basic Books, 1994), 33–35.

11. John Addington Symonds, *The Memoirs of John Addington Symonds,* ed. Phyllis Grosskurth (Chicago: University of Chicago Press, 1984), in Nye *Sexuality,* 157.

12. Ibid., 160.

13. For a fine general account of late nineteenth-century gay aesthetic subculture, see Richard Dellamora, *Masculine Desire: The Sexual Politics of Victorian Aestheticism* (Chapel Hill: University of North Carolina Press, 1990).

14. Walter Pater, *The Renaissance: Studies in Art and Poetry.* 1893. Ed. Donald J. Hill (Berkeley: University of California Press, 1980). See especially the essays "The Poetry of Michelangelo" and "Winckelmann."

15. Plato, *Symposium,* 181d.

16. For a detailed, if controversial biography of Wilde, see Richard Ellmann, *Oscar Wilde* (New York: Vintage, 1988).

17. For contemporary images of Wilde and of his trial, see "The trials of Oscar Wilde," www.law.umkc.edu.

18. For a discussion of how artists and poets sought to remain manly in the Victorian period, see Sussman, *Victorian Masculinities.*

19. *New York Times,* June 30 2011, A1.

20. Alfred Kinsey, *Sexual Behavior in the Human Male* (Philadelphia: W B. Saunders Company, 1948). Nye, *Sexuality,* 346.

21. Ibid., 346–47.

22. Ibid., 347.

23. Ibid.

24. Ibid., 346.

25. Chauncey, *Gay New York,* 13.

26. Freud, *Three Essays,* 186.

27. *New York Times,* June 30, 2011, B15.

28. Eve Kosofsky Sedgwick, *Epistemology of the Closet* (Berkeley: University of California Press, 1990), 185.

Conclusion

1. For a fine discussion of the contemporary pressures on a man's life, see Susan Faludi, *Stiffed: The Betrayal of the American Man* (New York: William Morrow, 1999).

2. Judith Halberstam, *Female Masculinity* (Durham, NC: Duke University Press, 1998), 1.

3. Ibid., 2.

4. Ibid.

Glossary

Note: These are not comprehensive definitions but specific ones that apply to the history of manliness.

agoge: system of rigorous military training for all male Spartans.

apprenticeship: long period of training in a craft under a master within the medieval guild system; more generally, a phase of early training for acquiring expertise in a craft.

arsenokoitēs: term used in the Christian Bible referring to those who engage in homosexual practices.

Arts and Crafts movement: late nineteenth-century movement in England, then spreading to America, advocating and practicing a return to handicraft in design and production; exemplified in activity of William Morris in England.

Ashkenazi: Eastern European Jews during the Jewish Diaspora; more specifically, Jews from the Jewish Pale of Settlement in what is now Russia, Poland, Ukraine, Lithuania, and Latvia who emigrated to America from the 1890s onward.

Athena: goddess of wisdom, patron of city-state of Athens; statue of Athena within the Parthenon.

banausoi: term applied in classical Athens to those who practiced *technē* or the practical work of making; this social class included craftsmen such as nail makers, tanners, and metalworkers as well as artisans such as goldsmiths and vase-painters, and those whom we today call architects.

battle rage: in combat, the loss of the rational self in a frenzy, often generating preternatural strength.

berdache: in many Native American tribes, a person considered of a third sex who contains the spirit of both the male and the female; often called a "two-spirit" person.

berserker: elite Viking warrior who experiences battle rage or *berserkergang*.

berserkergang: frenzy and fury in battle experienced by berserkers; see "battle rage."

breadwinner: in capitalist industrial society, the identity of a middle-class or working-class man whose principal responsibility is supporting his family through hard work.

bromance: contemporary term for affection between men not manifested in sexual activity.

Bushido: warrior code of Japanese samurai.

cash-nexus: relationship between people based solely on impersonal monetary transactions; a primary form of relation between a factory owner and his employee within industrial capitalism.

chattel slavery: form of servitude wherein the slave is the personal property or chattel of the slaveholder; slave owner is entitled to the full rewards of a slave's labor; slave can be bought and sold as a commodity; written into law as applying to blacks in the South in antebellum America.

chivalry: code of the medieval Christian warrior knight; now more generally a term for courtesy to women.

citizen-army: defense force composed of all able-bodied citizens; distinct from an all-volunteer army or army of mercenaries; usually composed of all male citizens, but can include both males and females as in contemporary Israel.

closet: metaphor for keeping one's homosexuality secret, as "in the closet"; also "closeted."

companionate marriage: marriage based on affection rather than on financial or dynastic considerations.

construction: idea that gender roles such as masculinity are shaped by society rather being the expression of innate or biological qualities; also constructivist, constructionism, and social construction.

continuum: a continuous series in distinction to dualisms categorizing irreconcilable oppositions, such as gay/straight.

craftsman: man whose primary self-definition as well as his definition by society depends upon his expert practice of making something well.

daimyo: feudal lord in Japan to whom a samurai pledged service and loyalty.

demos: body of Athenian citizens collectively; also the Assembly of Athenian citizens that voted on such matters as laws and government appointments.

diaspora: dispersion of a people from their ancestral homeland as in the Black Diaspora from Africa and the Jewish Diaspora from Palestine; also diasporic.

Discobolus: the discus-thrower; fifth century BCE statue by Myron of a nude male athlete in act of throwing a discus; manifested the ideal of classical Greek manliness.

dualism: opposition between two distinct entities; for example, male/female or straight/gay.

economic man: conception of man as an individual whose primary identity lies in the rational pursuit for himself of financial gain in the marketplace.

energistic theory: model explaining human action as the expression of energy developed within the body.

ephebe: Athenian youth between the ages of eighteen and twenty.

ephebeia: compulsory military training institution for Athenian youths (*ephebes*).

erastes: adolescent youth in Athens participating in the homoerotic relation with the adult male citizen (*eromenos*).

eromenos: adult citizen of Athens participating in homoerotic relation with the adolescent (*erastes*).

essentialism: idea that human qualities are innate rather than constructed by society.

fairy: an effeminate working-class male prostitute in late nineteenth-century New York City; continued in use, often in a pejorative sense, for homosexuals.

female masculinity: form of masculinity in which traditional masculine qualities are performed by female-born persons.

fugitive slave laws: laws in pre-Civil War America based on the idea of slaves as property; allowed slave owners to capture slaves who escaped into free states and return them to slavery.

gender: socially constructed expectations for behavior by persons of a specific sex; contrast to "sex" as the biological definition of male or female.

ghetto: area of city in which Jews are required to live; derived from *the Ghetto Nuova* island of Venice where Jews were confined in Middle Ages; more generally, an area in which a minority or oppressed group is confined.

guild: in Middle Ages, an association of artisans in the same craft formed to maintain standards of training and practice, and to uphold mutual interests; expanded to apply to groupings with mutual interests formed to protect those interests.

hara-kari: see *seppuku.*

Hasidic Jews: form of Orthodoxy developed in eighteenth-century Eastern Europe marked by devotion to a dynastic leader, wearing of distinctive clothing, and a greater than average study of the spiritual aspects of Torah; a number of Hasidic groups such as the Lubavitch and Satmar are now centered in Brooklyn, NY.

hegemonic masculinity: dominant form of masculinity or manliness within a society that contains many forms of manliness.

helots: large population enslaved in Sparta to perform labor shunned by the warrior citizens; more generally used to describe slaves.

Hephaestus: Greek god of metalworking and of craft in general; physically deformed, he was cuckolded by Ares who slept with Hephaestus's wife, Venus.

hermaphrodite: traditional term for a person having both male and female sexual characteristics and organs; now often called an intersex person.

heterosexual: term invented in late nineteenth century to describe what was seen as a totalizing masculine identity determined by opposite-sex desire; invented as the opposite of the homosexual as an identity.

homoerotic: describing sexual desire for a person of the same sex.

homophobia: attitude of hatred and fear of those men and women who feel homoerotic desire and/or engage in same-sex practices.

homosexual: term invented in the late nineteenth century to describe what was seen as a totalizing masculine identity determined by same-sex desire; as adjective, denotes such desire.

homosexual panic: acute anxiety experienced about acknowledging hidden homoerotic desire and/or having such desire revealed so as to be categorized as a homosexual.

homosocial: referring to the close male-male bonds not of a sexual nature; also homosociality.

homosocial continuum: continuity between homosocial and homosexual relations between men.

hoplite: Spartan and Athenian foot soldier; usually operating in phalanx formation.

human motor: male body conceived as an engine or motor expending energy from food consumed as fuel.

hybrid: group or a person in which different cultures and traditions mingle and interact; also hybridity.

identity: sense of self; created both internally and by affiliating with other men in a larger social construction.

Iliad: epic in oral form traditionally attributed to Homer describing siege of Troy by a coalition of Greek states; origin of poem most likely in eighth century BCE.

innateness: idea that human characteristics such as gender are inborn, biological rather than constructed by society.

intersex: contemporary term for person combining male and female sexual characteristics and organs; often used in place of the traditional term hermaphrodite.

Kinsey scale: seven-point scale employed by sex researcher Alfred Kinsey to measure same-sex desire in men; at one end those who had "no psychic responses to individuals of their own sex"; at the other end are those whose "more overt activity and/or psychic reactions" were "exclusively homosexual"; at the midpoint, those who are "equally homosexual and heterosexual in their overt experience and/or their psychic responses."

Labouchere Amendment: addition to the English Criminal Code in 1885 named after its sponsor that criminalized any act of "gross indecency" between men; Oscar Wilde was prosecuted under this vague law.

libido: term used by Freud to describe instinctual psychic energy; also as sexual desire undifferentiated at birth in terms of object choice.

male: person born biologically male as opposed to female; also used to describe behavior of males attributed to innate biological qualities.

male-born person: person born biologically male; distinct from a person medically reshaped to be a biological male.

manhood: state of achieving and continuing the ideal behaviors prescribed by society for adult men.

manliness: quality of performing the script set by society for male behavior.

masculinist: advocating male superiority and dominance.

masculinity: ideal script set for men by society; also "masculinities" as the plural to indicate the various forms that masculinity may take.

medicalization: process by which human conditions and problems come to be defined and treated as medical conditions or diseases and thus come under the authority of doctors and other health professionals.

mensch: Yiddish term of value for a "real man"; expression of high praise for one who is morally responsible and committed to his work, to his religion, and to his family.

metrosexual: urban heterosexual male preoccupied with fashion and his personal style.

middle-class morality: ethos developed by the bourgeois; includes sexual puritanism, compulsory marriage, and the work ethic.

molly houses: eighteenth-century gathering places in England where self-identified gay men or mollies congregated; evidence of an early gay subculture.

monetize: to convert something into value as money.

Nation of Islam: African-American religious organization founded in 1930; led for many years by Elijah Muhammad; advocates black separatism; Malcolm X active in organization until splitting with its leadership.

naturalizing: attributing socially constructed phenomena to nature, to being natural; akin to innateness and essentialism.

negritude: innate qualities of aesthetics and consciousness in blacks; from anti-colonial movement of 1930s asserting the value of these essential qualities in black people.

normalization: term used by Zionists for the effort to have Jewish Diaspora masculinity conform to normal or normative Western masculine ideals.

normative: term used to describe what society constructs as the norm; differs from "normal," which suggests an essentialist vision.

paideia: ideal quality of mind created by the Athenian system of a liberal education for the citizen.

palaestra: outdoor space in ancient Athens set aside for physical training.

Pale of Settlement: often "Jewish Pale of Settlement"; area now comprising parts of Russia, Poland, Ukraine, Latvia, and Lithuania to which Jews were in 1791 confined by law; region from which many Jews emigrated to America in the late nineteenth and early twentieth centuries.

Parthenon: temple built in fifth century BCE Athens to house statue of city's patron goddess Athena; emblematic structure of this high civilization.

passionate friendship: nineteenth-century term for intense nonsexual male-male bonding.

patriarchal: describes a social structure in which men hold all positions of power and, more specifically, power over women.

performative: idea that gender is the performance or playing out in public of a script constructed by society; contrasts with idea of gender as the expression of innate qualities.

perversion: term invented by late nineteenth-century sexologists for any seemingly abnormal sexual practice; specifically for acts that deviate from what is considered natural or healthy heterosexual genital sex.

phalanx: Greek formation of armed infantry in close deep ranks and files in which each hoplite is guarded by the shields of another man.

philia: Greek term for intense nonsexual love; applies to such love between men but can apply to other relations.

polis: term applied both to Athens as a city-state and to its citizens as an entity, especially in performing democratic duties in the Assembly such as voting for laws and appointing government and military leaders.

polymorphous: deriving sexual pleasure from any part of the body in non-normative sexual activity; in psychoanalytic terminology often as "polymorphous perversity."

post-black: similar to post-racial to describe time in which black people are no longer judged by race.

post-racial: term for a society in which considerations of race are no longer relevant.

Protestant ethic: belief derived from Calvinism that working hard and success in one's worldly calling are signs of an individual's election to eternal salvation; also termed "work ethic."

PTSD: Post-Traumatic Stress Disorder; an anxiety disorder that can develop after exposure to a terrifying event or ordeal in which grave physical harm occurred or was threatened, such as military combat.

Rabbinic Judaism: form of Judaism developed after the destruction of the Second Temple in 70 CE; worship takes place in a synagogue containing the sacred scroll or Torah and is led by a learned man or rabbi.

Reconstruction: period from 1865 to approximately 1877 during which the North attempted to reshape or reconstruct the defeated Confederacy; characterized by efforts to provide education, land, and voting rights to emancipated slaves; eventually failed as North lost interest, and Southern whites reasserted racial domination.

ronin: samurai knights without a master.

samurai: caste of warriors in Japan from 794–1868; famous for skill with the sword, for following strict warrior code of Bushido, and for loyalty to a master.

self-help: nineteenth-century doctrine of radical individualism devoted to economic gain and social mobility; term from best-selling book by Samuel Smiles, *Self-Help: with Illustrations of Character and Conduct* (1859).

self-made man: man who has risen from low social rank through his own efforts; in distinction to a man who possesses wealth and position through inheritance or through the rank of his birth family.

Semper Fidelis: Latin for "always faithful"; motto of the United States Marine Corps; often shortened to "semper fi."

separatism: movement advocating separation from a larger group or political unit; as in black separatism in America.

Sephardic Jews: descendants of Jews who left Spain or Portugal after the 1492 expulsion from these lands; earliest Jews in America were Sephardim who immigrated via Latin America and the Caribbean.

seppuku: also known as hari-kari; ceremonial suicide by a samurai to preserve his honor; performed by cutting abdomen open with his short knife (*wakizashi*).

sex: male or female as defined by biology; contrast to gender as the social construction of what is appropriate for each sex.

sexologist: person working in the field of sexology.

sexology: field applying the methods of science to sexual desire and sexual practices; developed in late nineteenth-century Europe.

shtetl: rural village to which Jews were confined in the Pale of Settlement.

sodomites: term applied to men who engaged in sexual acts with other men; derived from biblical story of the destruction of the city of Sodom because its inhabitants purportedly engaged in same-sex practices.

sodomy: general and often vague term for nonnormative sexual practices, such as oral and anal sex; often applied specifically to male-male sex; derived from biblical story of the destruction of the city of Sodom because its inhabitants performed such acts.

spermatic energy: nineteenth-century term for what was seen as a vital power in males that derives from seminal fluid; also spermatic economy as discourse dealing with the regulation of male energy in the production and ejaculation or spending of seminal fluid.

social construction: see "construction."

symposium: drinking party for men in classical Athens; Plato's *The Symposium* describes such an event at which man-boy erotics was discussed.

technē: Greek term denoting the application of skill to shaping material forms; based on distinction between doing and knowing.

third sex: a sex that that cannot be categorized as male nor female; used, for example, in late nineteenth-century Europe for men feeling desire for other men or for the berdache in some Native American cultures.

transgender: umbrella term used to describe people whose gender identity (sense of themselves as male or female) differs from that usually associated with their birth sex.

transsexual: person who seeks to live or does live as a member of the opposite sex particularly by undergoing surgery and hormone therapy.

two-sex model: belief that only two sexes exist, male and female.

Uranians: name adopted by elite late nineteenth-century men in England who felt homoerotic desire; derived from Greek goddess Urania praised as patron of man-boy erotics in Plato's *The Symposium*.

wakizashi: short knife used by samurai for battle and for the ceremony of *seppuku*.

work ethic: see "Protestant ethic."

yeshiva: Jewish religious school devoted to study of sacred texts.

Bibliography

Adams, Rachel, and David Savran, eds. *The Masculinity Studies Reader.* Malden, MA: Blackwell, 2002. Fine collection of theoretical and descriptive essays dealing with varied forms of manliness.

Ambrose, Steven E. *Band of Brothers: E Company, 506th Regiment, 101st Airborne from Normandy to Hitler's Eagle's Nest.* New York: Simon & Schuster, 2001.

Babel, Isaac. *Isaac Babel: Collected Stories.* Ed. Nathalie Babel. Trans. Peter Constantine. New York: Penguin, 1994.

Beard, Mary. *Pompeii.* London: Profile Books, 2008. Account of life in this Roman city with attention to the social position and activities of craftsmen.

Boyarin, Daniel. *Unheroic Conduct: The Rise of Heterosexuality and the Invention of the Jewish Man.* Berkeley: University of California Press, 1997.

Burford, Alison. *Craftsmen in Greek and Roman Society.* Ithaca, NY: Cornell University Press, 1972. Fine detailed account of the status and activities of the craftsman in the classical world.

Butler, Judith. *Gender Trouble.* New York: Routledge, 1999.

Carlyle, Thomas. *Past and Present.* 1843. Boston: Houghton Mifflin, 1965. Classic Victorian statement of how obedience to the work ethic engenders manliness in the industrial world.

Chauncey, George. *Gay New York: Gender, Urban Culture, and the Making of the Gay Male World, 1890–1940.* New York: Basic Books, 1995. Rich and definitive account of the varied forms of gay life in the city within this period.

Chernow, Ron. *Washington: A Life.* New York: Penguin, 2010. Kindle edition.

Clark, Kenneth. *The Nude: A Study in Ideal Form.* New York: Anchor, 1956.

Cohen, Rich. *Tough Jews: Fathers, Sons, and Gangster Dreams.* New York: Vintage, 1999.

Dellamora, Richard. *Masculine Desire: The Sexual Politics of Victorian Aestheticism.* Chapel Hill: University of North Carolina Press, 1990.

Dickens, Charles. *A Christmas Carol.* 1843. Bantam: New York, 1986.

Dickens, Charles. *Great Expectations.* 1861. London: Penguin, 2002.

Douglass, Frederick. *Narrative of the Life of Frederick Douglass, an American Slave.* 1845. New York: Barnes & Noble, 2003.

Ellmann, Richard. *Oscar Wilde.* New York: Vintage, 1988. Definitive, if controversial, biography.

Emerson, Ralph Waldo. "Hymn: Sung at the Completion of the Concord Monument," in *American Poetry: The Nineteenth Century,* vol. 1, ed. John Hollander. New York: New American Library, 1993, 318–19.

Emerson, Ralph Waldo. "Self-Reliance." 1841. Reprinted www.gutenberg.org/files/16643/16643-h/16643-h.htm.

Eugenides, Jeffrey. *Middlesex.* New York: Picador, 2007.

Faludi, Susan. *Stiffed: The Betrayal of the American Man.* New York: William Morrow, 1999. Fine analysis of the contemporary pressures on men, with emphasis on economic causes.

Fanon, Frantz. *Black Skin, White Masks,* in Adams, *Masculinity Reader,* 232–44.

Fausto-Sterling, Anne. "How to Build a Man," in Nye, *Sexuality,* 234–39. Fine account of the problems of categorizing sex within the two-sex model.

Fausto-Sterling, Anne. "The Sexe Which Prevaileth," in Adams, *Masculinity Studies,* 375–88. Excellent account of the cultural issues past and present concerning intersex persons.

Fitzgerald, F. Scott. *The Great Gatsby.* 1925. Reprinted in *Three Novels of F. Scott Fitzgerald.* New York: Scribner's, 1953.

Foner, Eric. *The Fiery Trial: Abraham Lincoln and American Slavery.* New York: Norton, 2010. The definitive treatment of the subject.

Ford, Ford Madox. *Ford Madox Brown: A Record of His Life and Work.* London: Longmans, 1896.

Foucault, Michel. *Herculine Barbin: Being the Recently Discovered Memoirs of a Nineteenth-Century French Hermaphrodite.* New York: Vintage, 1980.

Foucault, Michel. *The History of Sexuality: Volume I: An Introduction.* New York: Vintage, 1990.

Freud, Sigmund. *Three Essays on the Theory of Sexuality,* trans. James Strachey. New York: Basic Books, 1962. In Nye, *Sexuality,* 185–92.

Gates, Henry Louis, Jr. *The Signifying Monkey: A Theory of African-American Literary Criticism.* New York: Oxford University Press, 1989. Account of the trickster figure in African-American literature.

Gilmore, David D. *Manhood in the Making: Cultural Concepts of Masculinity.* New Haven, CT: Yale University Press, 1990.

Halberstam, Judith. *Female Masculinity.* Durham, NC: Duke University Press, 1998. Influential argument for a form of masculinity in which traditional masculine qualities are performed by female-born persons.

Haley, Alex. *Roots: The Saga of an American Family.* Garden City, NY: Doubleday, 1976.

Hollander, John, ed. *American Poetry: The Nineteenth Century,* vol. 1. New York: Library of America, 1993.

Homer. "Hymn to Hephaestus." http://ancienthistory.about.com/library/bl/bl_text_homerhymn_hephaestus.htm.

Homer. *The Iliad.* Trans. Robert Fagles. New York, Penguin, 1990.

Jaeger, Werner. *Paideia: the Ideals of Greek Culture.* New York: Oxford University Press, 1945. The definitive account of the Athenian humanistic ideal.

Junger, Ernst. *Storm of Steel.* 1920. New York: Penguin, 2004.

Kagan, Donald. *Pericles of Athens and the Birth of Democracy.* New York: Free Press, 1991. Clear account of Pericles as an exemplary democratic man.

Kingston, Maxine Hong. *The Woman Warrior: Memoirs of a Girlhood among Ghosts.* New York: Vintage, 1989.

Kinsey, Alfred. *Sexual Behavior in the Human Male.* Philadelphia: W. B. Saunders Company, 1948. In Nye, *Sexuality,* 345–47.

Kulick, Don. "The Gender of Brazilian Transgendered Prostitutes," in Adams, *Masculinity Reader,* 389–407.

Laquer, Thomas. *Making Sex: Body and Gender from the Greeks to Freud.* Cambridge: Harvard University Press, 1992. Fine account of the history of the two-sex model, as well as other models for categorizing sexes.

Malcolm X. *The Autobiography of Malcolm X.* 1964. New York: Ballantine, 1973.

Mishima, Yukio. *Patriotism.* New York: New Directions, 2010.

Morrison, Toni. *Beloved.* New York: Columbia University Press, 1998.

New York Plumbers Local Union 1. www.ualocal1.org.

Nye, Robert, ed. *Sexuality.* Oxford, UK: Oxford University Press, 1999.

Obama, Barack. *Dreams from My Father: A Story of Race and Inheritance.* New York: Times Books, 1995.

O'Brien, Tim. "The Things They Carried," in *The Norton Anthology of Short Fiction: Shorter Seventh Edition,* ed. Richard Bausch. New York: Norton, 2006. 603–15.

Orwell, George. *1984.* 1949. New York: Signet, 1949.

Pater, Walter. *The Renaissance: Studies in Art and Poetry.* 1893. Ed. Donald J. Hill. Berkeley: University of California Press, 1980.

Paterson, Orlando. "Race Unbound." Review of *Who's Afraid of Post-Blackness,* by Touré. *New York Times Sunday Book Review.* September 25, 2011.

Pericles, "Funeral Oration." www.fordham.edu/halsall/ancient/pericles-funeral-speech.html. Eulogy at the funeral of Athenians who died in the war against Sparta; eloquent statement of the lineaments of Athenian manhood.

Pinckney, Darryl. "The Two Conversions of Malcolm X." Review of *Malcolm X: A Life of Reinvention,* by Manning Marable. *The New York Review of Books.* 58: September 29, 2011.

Plato. *The Symposium.* New York: Penguin, 1999.

Plutarch, *On Sparta.* Richard Talbert, ed. London: Penguin, 2005.

Rabinbach, Anson. *The Human Motor: Energy, Fatigue, and the Origins of Modernity.* Berkeley: University of California Press, 1992. The definitive account of the nineteenth-century reconceptualization of the male body as an engine.

Roisman, Joseph. *The Rhetoric of Manhood: Masculinity in the Attic Orators.* Berkeley: University of California Press, 2005. Fine account of the ideals of manliness in ancient Athens as represented in contemporary speeches.

Roth, Philip. *Goodbye Columbus and Five Short Stories*. 1959. New York: Vintage, 1994.

Rotundo, Anthony. *American Manhood: Transformations in Masculinity from the Revolution to the Modern Era*. New York: Basic Books, 1994. General study of cultural changes in manliness throughout the history of America.

Ruskin, John. "The Nature of Gothic." 1851–53. In *The Norton Anthology of English Literature*. New York: Norton, 2000. 2:1432–42. This section of his multivolume *The Stones of Venice* provides the most eloquent and influential nineteenth-century account of the necessity of craft work for spiritual well-being.

Russo, Richard. "High and Dry." *Granta*, no. 111 (2010). A family memoir describing the destruction of a community of craftsmen devoted to the making of gloves by the introduction of glove-making machinery.

Sedgwick, Eve Kosofsky. *Between Men: English Literature and Male Homosocial Desire*. New York: Columbia University Press, 1985. Influential discussion of the homosocial continuum.

Sedgwick, Eve Kosofsky. *Epistemology of the Closet*. Berkeley: University of California Press, 1990. Perceptive and influential account of the effects of the closeting of homosexuals.

Sennett, Richard. *The Craftsman*. New York: Penguin, 2009. A persuasive argument for the definition of craft as expertise in the present day and for the continued importance of working with the hand for mental well-being.

Shay, Jonathan. *Achilles in Vietnam: Combat Trauma and the Undoing of Character*. New York: Simon & Schuster, 1994. Brilliant account by a psychiatrist comparing the modes of engaging trauma in *The Iliad* and in the Vietnam War.

Showalter, Elaine. *Sexual Anarchy: Gender and Culture at the Fin de Siècle*. New York: Viking, 1990.

Smiles, Samuel. *Self-Help: with Illustrations of Character and Conduct*. 1859. London: IEA Health and Welfare Unit, 1996.

Stearns, Peter. *Be a Man!: Males in Modern Society*. Teaneck, NJ: Holmes & Meier, 1990. General history of manliness.

Sussman, Herbert. *Victorian Masculinities: Manhood and Masculine Poetics in Early Victorian Literature and Art*. Cambridge: Cambridge University Press, 1995. The varied forms of manliness in nineteenth-century England with emphasis on the vexed relation of manliness to the making of literature and art.

Sussman, Herbert. *Victorian Technology: Invention, Innovation, and the Rise of the Machine*. Santa Barbara, CA: Praeger, 2009. The advent of mechanization in the nineteenth century and its effect on the identity of the craftsman.

Suzuki, Daisetz Teitaro. *Zen and Japanese Culture*. Princeton, NJ: Princeton University Press, 1938.

Symonds, John Addington. *The Memoirs of John Addington Symonds*. 1893. Ed. Phyllis Grosskurth. Chicago: University of Chicago Press, 1984. In Nye, *Sexuality*, 157–60.

Touré, *Who's Afraid of Post-Blackness*. New York: Free Press, 2011.

Twain, Mark. *Adventures of Huckleberry Finn*. 1884. etext.virginia.edu/twain/huck-finn.html.

U.S. Marine Corps official website. www.marines.com.

Washington, George. "Letter to Touro Synagogue." 1790. www.tourosynagogue. org/pdfs/WashingtonLetter.pdf.

Whitman, Walt. *Leaves of Grass*. Ed. Sculley Bradley and Harold Blodgett. New York: Norton, 1973.

Wilde, Oscar. "The Ballad of Reading Gaol." 1898. In *The Portable Oscar Wilde*. New York, Penguin, 1981.

Wilde, Oscar. *The Importance of Being Earnest*. 1893. In *The Portable Oscar Wilde*.

Wilde, Oscar. *The Picture of Dorian Gray*. 1890. In *The Portable Oscar Wilde*.

Wills, Gary. *Lincoln at Gettysburg: The Words that Remade America*. New York: Simon & Schuster, 1992.

Wilson, William Scott. *Ideals of the Samurai: Writings of Japanese Warriors*. New York: Black Belt Communications, 1982.

Wright, Richard. *Black Boy*. 1954. In *Richard Wright: Works*. New York: Library of America, 1991.

Filmography

Annie Hall. Dir. Woody Allen. Perf. Diane Keaton, Woody Allen. MGM, 1977.

Butch Cassidy and the Sundance Kid. Dir. George Roy Hill. Perf. Paul Newman, Robert Redford, and Katherine Ross. Twentieth Century Fox, 1969.

Crouching Tiger, Hidden Dragon (Wo hu cang long). Dir. Ang Lee. Perf. Yun-Fat Chow, Michelle Yeoh. Asia Union, 2000.

Fight Club. Dir. David Fincher. Perf. Brad Pitt, Edward Norton. Fox 2000, 1999.

The Full Monty. Dir. Peter Cattaneo. Perf. Robert Carlyle, Tom Wilkinson. Redwave, 1997.

Go Tell the Spartans. Dir. Ted Post. Perf. Burt Lancaster, Craig Wasson. Mar Vista, 1978.

I Love you Man. Dir. John Hamburg. Perf. Paul Rudd, Jason Segel. DreamWorks, 2009.

The Magnificent Seven. Dir. John Stevens. Perf. Yul Brynner, Steve McQueen. Mirisch, 1954.

Old Joy. Dir. Kelly Reichardt. Perf. Daniel London, Will Oldham. Film Science, 2006.

Patton. Dir. Franklin Schaffner. Perf. George C. Scott, Karl Malden. Twentieth Century Fox, 1970.

Restropo. Dir. Tim Hetherington, Sebastian Junger. Outpost, 2011.

Seven Samurai (Shichenin no Samurai). Dir. Akira Kurosawa. Perf. Toshirô Mifune. Toho, 1954.

Index

About the Author

HERBERT SUSSMAN is professor emeritus of English at Northeastern University, Boston, Massachusetts; and an adjunct faculty member at The New School, New York, New York. He has also taught at the University of California, Berkeley. Sussman is the author of *Victorian Masculinities: Manhood and Masculine Poetics in Early Victorian Literature and Art*; *Victorian Technology: Invention, Innovation, and the Rise of the Machine*; and various essays on the construction of masculinity.